**SECOND EDITION**

# START YOUR OWN
# SENIOR
# HOME CARE
# BUSINESS

## CRAIG WALLIN

**Second Edition**

**Start Your Own
Senior Home Care Business**

Copyright © 2020 by Craig Wallin
All Rights Reserved

Headstartpublishing.com

## Dedication

If you've been downsized, outsourced, grown tired of the rat race or just need more income and a brighter future, this book is for you. If you're ready to take charge and become your own boss, this book is for you.

Since I published the first edition of this guide, I've heard from many readers who have started their own profitable local senior home care businesses. I'm thankful they have shared their stories, because their contributions have made this second edition a bigger, better and more useful guide. Thank you all!

Thanks for buying this guidebook and may your new senior home care business thrive and prosper!

# Table of Contents

# Introduction

10,000 baby boomers a day will turn 65 in America every single day between now and the year 2030. By 2030, there will be over 70 million Americans over 65. That's one out of every five Americans!

Those older folks will live longer and have more money to spend, thanks to an era of prosperity during their working years. Over 80 percent of seniors own their own homes, and plan to stay in them as long as possible.

But with age can come chronic health conditions or temporary medical emergencies, like a disabling fall, that may require assistance to remain at home. To provide assistance to this rapidly growing population of seniors requires an army of senior care providers, who can help with everyday in-home chores that may be difficult or impossible for many seniors, like meal preparation, light housekeeping, shopping and errands or help with bathing and dressing.

Often as little as 3 hours of help every day can enable seniors to remain in their own home longer, which is the preferred choice for 90 percent of them. At home, they are able to maintain their privacy, dignity and independence.

In addition, staying in their own home with some regular assistance from a senior home care provider is actually more cost effective than nursing home care, so it makes financial sense as well. A recent cost of care survey found the average daily cost of nursing home care was $260 a day, while in-home care averaged $150 a day.

Staying at home also benefits the children of seniors, the "sandwich generation," who also have to work and raise their own children. With help from a senior care provider, visits to their parents can be more about quality time together rather than having so many responsibilities to deal with at every visit. This is much less stressful for both seniors and their adult children.

Because of the rapid growth in the senior population, home care services are the fastest growing part of the entire health care industry in America. Advances in medical technology and treatment have made it possible for more people to be cared for at home instead of at a hospital or nursing home.

Also, increasing health care costs are fueling the growing demand for more affordable in- home care. It's a lot more cost-effective to leave a hospital sooner or avoid a nursing home stay if all a senior requires is assistance with daily activities.

A non-medical senior home care business is much easier to start than a home health care business, because it doesn't require skilled caregivers, such as nurses. This is why only 28 states out of 50 currently have licensing and registration requirements for starting a non- medical home care business.

Another good reason to start your own senior health care business is that your customers are mostly private clients paying out-of-pocket for services. Unlike payments from Medicaid and long-term care insurance companies, private pay rates are higher and it's far easier to get paid promptly. According to the Private Duty Industry Report, over 80 percent of payments for non-medical home care come from private-pay clients, such as seniors or their adult children.

## How Much Can I Earn?

Rates for private senior home care providers range from $30 to $60 per hour nationally. Rates are higher in large cities and lower in smaller towns and rural areas where the cost of living is lower.

By starting your own senior home care business, you can charge the "retail" rates in your area – a big jump from the much lower wage paid to employees. Here's how it works:

Let's say the average wage in your area for a senior caregiver is $15 per hour through an agency. The employer adds their "markup" for administrative overhead and a profit margin, which brings the hourly rate billed to a client to $30 an hour. Which would you rather earn - $15 or $30?

With rates of $30 to $60 per hour of billable time, you can see it's possible to earn a solid income of $60,000 to $120,000 per year, depending on the rates where you live.

Best of all, senior care is a recession-proof business. People grow old and require in-home care regardless of what the national economy is doing. In addition, there is no expensive training or college classes required, as you can earn while you learn.

## Are You Ready?

Before making the decision to start your own senior home care business, it's wise to take a good look at your personal strengths and weaknesses to see if this business really makes sense for you. Consider asking your spouse or partner as well. Here are the questions you need to ask yourself:

1. Are you a caring, compassionate person? Your clients will be senior citizens with health conditions who require patience and understanding. Also, because they are home-bound, they may be socially isolated and need a friendly listener and a cheerful smile.

2. Are you an energetic person? Whether you are a "lone eagle" or managing several hired care providers, running a business is hard work. You need to be ready to work occasional 12-hour days, pull an unexpected shift when a caregiver calls in sick, and answer phone calls from clients, employees and prospects day or night.

3. Are you motivated? You will need to stay motivated after the initial excitement of launching your new business wears off and the day-to-day grind sets in. Of course, knowing you're the boss now, and are earning an independent, growing income will help strengthen your motivation!

4. Are you organized? Being able to manage your time, your employee's time and all the other aspects of your new business are critical to your success. You'll find tips and advice in the chapters that follow that help you to get – and stay – organized so you can get more done in less time with less stress.

5. Are you a people person? A senior home care business is all about people, from clients to employees to prospects

and others you'll manage from time to time. If you'd rather be playing video games than meeting a new person, you may want to consider another business. But if you can handle the occasional cranky employee or client and keep smiling, you'll do well providing home care.

6. Are you a self-starter? When you start your own business, it's up to you to make things happen. There is no more boss to turn to – it's just you and another deadline or appointment. From scheduling to organizing, you're in charge, and the project won't get done until you dig in and do it! Again – the rewards are great – for example, when you land a new client or get a grateful note from a client's kids who love what you've done for their mother or dad.

# CHAPTER ONE

# What is Senior Home Care?

Most senior home care clients are between 65 and 95 years old, living in their own home, who just need help with daily living activities. They may have chronic health conditions such as memory loss, arthritis or heart disease, that limit their activities.

There are two types of senior home care, medical home care, often called home health care, and non-medical home care. Home health care services are ordered by a doctor and are provided by nurses or other trained medical personnel, such as respiratory care therapists, and are strictly regulated by state agencies.

Non-medical home care is much less restricted and involves services such as laundry, meal preparation, housekeeping, errands, bathing, dressing, transportation and medication reminders.

## Typical Non-Medical Services

**Bathing, Dressing & Grooming ...** A shower can be a dangerous place for a senior, as the fall risk is high. Often, fear of falling can keep seniors from bathing as often as they should. Just being there to help a senior in and out of the shower or tub is reassuring.

Arthritic joints in older folks can make buttons and even zippers a challenge. A senior care provider can help with these activities and boost a senior's self –esteem while doing so.

**Companionship ...** A senior's adult children may have a busy life or live far away, which can cause feelings of isolation or even depression. A senior care provider can help by simply being there to lend a sympathetic ear or get them out of the house to visit friends or do a bit of shopping. Many seniors with failing vision enjoy having a book read to them, or even having their caregiver check out audiobooks from the library. Playing cards or board games is another popular activity.

**Laundry ...** Seniors may neglect this seemingly simple task because they forget or it's just too much work, especially changing the bed linens.

**Light Housekeeping ...** Like laundry, keeping up with dusting, vacuuming and mopping may be too much work for many seniors, and impaired vision may also make it more difficult. If a more thorough cleaning is needed, a senior care provider can contact a professional cleaning service.

**Meal Preparation ...** Healthy eating is an important part of healthy aging, and many seniors neglect their nutritional needs as it's "too much work," opting instead to just open a can or pop a TV dinner in their microwave. A senior care provider can make sure any dietary restrictions are followed, and cook healthy, nutritious meals, with generous portions to provide leftovers for another day.

**Medication Reminders ...** Seniors care providers can help with self-administered medications by reminding clients to take their meds. This can help avoid skipping a dose, taking the wrong medication, or taking an extra dose because they forgot if they took it earlier. A non-medical care provider is not permitted to actually administer the medication.

**Respite Care ...** Many families need temporary relief, also called respite care. Outside caregivers can provide a break for family members to allow time away from full-time care giving. While they take a break, their loved ones can continue to get dependable assistance and companionship.

**Safeguard Visits ...** Many seniors do not require daily assistance with everyday activities like meal preparation or bathing. Often a regular scheduled visit once or twice a week to check to make sure everything is okay will suffice.

This safeguard visit is especially appreciated by a senior's adult children, who often live too far away to visit frequently, but still want to make sure their parent is doing well. A checklist is used at each visit to ensure nothing is overlooked, and usually includes:

- ✓ Checking food supply and possible food spoilage.
- ✓ Brief home safety check to prevent falls.
- ✓ Bring in mail or newspapers.
- ✓ Remove trash.
- ✓ Medication reminders.
- ✓ Check and adjust room temperatures.
- ✓ Assist with apparel selection if needed.
- ✓ Companionship & conversation.

See chapter four for more information on safeguard visits.

**Shopping & Errands ...** Many home care clients require help with errands, such as picking up prescriptions, groceries or mail. As most are unable to drive, senior care providers can help by driving them to doctor's appointments, church, shopping or social activities. Do not use your own vehicle to transport a client unless you have the required special licensing and insurance. Most clients still have their own vehicle to use and just need a capable driver.

**Other Services ...**

- ✓ Answer the phone or read mail.
- ✓ Daily phone call to check on client.
- ✓ Lawn mowing and watering.
- ✓ Organize closets.
- ✓ Bill paying, and appointment scheduling.

# CHAPTER TWO

# Setting Up Your Senior Home Care Business

If you've honestly answered yes to most of the questions in the last chapter, it's time to get started. Before you can legally start your new business, there are several steps you'll need to complete. Here are the basic requirements:

- ✓ Choose your legal form of business.
- ✓ Pick a business name.
- ✓ Obtain a tax ID number and business licenses.
- ✓ Business insurance.
- ✓ Set up a bank account.
- ✓ Set up a record-keeping system.

Many private senior home care providers are "lone eagles," and prefer to keep their business small and simple. Others, attracted to the higher income potential, hire employees to do most of the actual in-home work and focus on managing the business.

While it's true a larger senior home care business can generate a substantial income, there is a lot of work involved. You have to hire and manage employees, handle endless administrative tasks, and spend less time out and about, actually helping senior clients. It's up to you to decide which direction to take. The majority of private senior care providers are small businesses, with one to ten employees.

**Legal form of business ...** If you intend to have no employees, a sole proprietorship makes sense. If you envision two or more partners, a partnership or limited liability corporation (LLC) could be a good choice. Most new small businesses are choosing the LLC format, as it's easy to set up (most states have free downloadable forms) and does not require a separate tax return to be filed.

**Sole Proprietorship ...** The easiest legal form of business to set up but has limited legal protection. The business operates under your personal social security number, and federal taxes are paid as part of your 1040 tax return.

**Limited Liability Corporation (LLC) ...** Popular because owners have limited personal liability, management flexibility and pass-through taxation (taxes are also paid as a part of your standard 1040 return.

To learn more about choosing the best legal structure for your new senior home care business, visit www.nolo.com, and click on "free legal information." Nolo can also help you properly establish a limited liability corporation in any state.

## Pick a business name

Start by making a list of several possible business names that best describe your new senior home care company. Be sure to pick a name that suggests what your company is all about, as that name is the first impression a prospective client will have.

For example, Dependable Home Care, or Dependable Caregivers tells a prospect what you do as well as suggesting that your company is dependable. Adding the name of your town tells prospects your service area, as well as make it easier for the search engines, such as Google, to find your web site when you set that up. Here are a few ideas to get you started:

- ✓ Senior Helpers
- ✓ Affordable Care
- ✓ Budget Caregivers
- ✓ Loving Caregivers
- ✓ Senior Care Angels

Be sure to choose a name that is easy to spell and remember. Before you make your final selection, get feedback from family or friends. Do they like it? Could it be improved?

After you've chosen a name, verify that you can use the name. Start by checking to see if the name can be registered as a domain name, as you'll need a website containing your company name to help customers and prospects contact you online and learn more about your services.

Next, check with your county clerk's office to see if your proposed business name is in use by anyone else. If you plan to use an LLC legal structure, check with your state's corporate filing office or Secretary of State.

Do a federal trademark search (free, at USPTO.gov) of the name you've chosen to ensure no one else is using the name, or if your use of the name would confuse someone, or if the name is "famous." For example, you wouldn't want to use the name

"Comfort Keepers of Ashland" because Comfort Keepers is a well-known national homecare brand name.

Now that you've made sure your chosen business name is available, it's time to register the name. In most cases, this is handled by your local county clerk's office.

## File for licenses and permits

Start with the IRS, as you'll need the "Employer Identification Number," or EIN, when you apply for other licenses, permits and a bank account. Visit the IRS web site at www.irs.gov and enter "Form SS4" in the search window.

Next, you can choose to print the application form out, or apply online. Applying online is much faster, and you can actually get your EIN when you've finished filling out the form!

After you have the EIN, apply for a local (city or county) business license. They may ask how many employees you intend to have. I suggest you tell them you will be the only one. If you plan to use a home office, they are concerned about traffic and parking issues. Just tell them that customers will never visit the office – it is only for management work, such as bookkeeping.

In many states, a home care business must apply for a specialized license. Currently only 28 of the 50 states require a specialized license, but you will need to contact your state to get the latest information. Here is a contact list for every state's health department's online address, where you can check the current requirements. If you are viewing the eBook, you can simply click the link to go to your state's web site.

- Alabama Dept. of Human Resources:
  www.dhr.state.al.us
- Alaska Dept. of Health & Social Services:
  www.hss.state.ak.us
- Arizona Dept. of Economic Security:
  www.azdes.gov
- Arkansas Dept. of Human Services:
  www.humanservices.arkansas.gov
- California Dept. of Social Services:
  www.dss.cahwnet.gov
- Colorado Dept. of Human Services:
  www.cdhs.state.co.us
- Connecticut Dept. of Social Services:
  www.ct.gov/dss/site/default.asp
- Delaware Dept. of Health & Social Services:
  www.dhss.delaware.gov/dhss
- District of Columbia Dept. of Human Services:
  www.dhs.dc.gov
- Florida Agency for Health Care Admin:
  www.fdhc.state.fl.us
- Georgia Dept. of Human Services:
  www.dhr.state.ga.us
- Hawaii Dept. of Human Services:
  www.hawaii.gov/dhs
- Idaho Dept. of Health & Welfare:
  www.healthandwelfare.idaho.gov
- Illinois Dept. of Human Services:
  www.dhs.state.il.us

- Indiana Family & Social Services:
  www.in.gov/fssa

- Iowa Dept. of Human Services:
  www.dhs.state.ia.us

- Kansas Dept. of Social & Rehabilitation Services:
  www.dcf.ks.gov

- Kentucky Dept of Health & Human Services:
  www.chfs.ky.gov

- Louisiana Dept. of Social Services:
  www.dss.state.la.us

- Maine Dept. of Health & Human Services:
  www.maine.gov/dhhs

- Maryland Dept. of Human Resources:
  www.dhr.state.md.us

- Massachusetts Dept. of Social Services:
  www.mass.gov/dss

- Michigan Dept. of Community Health:
  www.michigan.gov/mdch

- Minnesota Dept. of Human Services:
  www.dhs.state.mn.us

- Mississippi Dept. of Human Services:
  www.mdhs.state.ms.us

- Missouri Dept. of Social Services:
  www.dss.mo.gov

- Montana Dept. of Health & Human Services:
  www.dphhs.mt.gov

- Nebraska Health & Human Services:
  www.dhhs.ne.gov

- Nevada Dept. of Human Resources:
  www.dhhs.nv.gov
- New Hampshire Dept. of Health & Human Services:
  www.dhhs.state.nh.us
- New Jersey Dept. of Human Services:
  www.state.nj.us/humanservices
- New Mexico Health & Human Services:
  www.hsd.state.nm.us
- New York State Family Services:
  www.homecare.nyhealth.gov
- North Carolina Dept. of Health & Human Services:
  www.dhhs.state.nc.us
- North Dakota Dept. of Human Services:
  www.dhs.nd.gov
- Ohio Dept. of Family Services:
  www.jfs.ohio.gov
- Oklahoma Dept. of Family Services:
  www.okdhs.org
- Oregon Dept. of Human Services:
  www.oregon.gov/DHS
- Pennsylvania Dept. of Public Welfare:
  www.dpw.state.pa.us
- Rhode Island Dept. of Human Services:
  www.dhs.ri.gov
- South Carolina Dept. of Health & Human Services:
  www.scdhhs.gov
- Tennessee Dept. of Human Services:
  www.state.tn.us/humanserv

- Texas Health & Human Services:
  www.hhsc.state.tx.us

- Utah Dept. of Human Services:
  www.dhs.state.ut.us

- Vermont Agency of Human Services:
  www.humanservices.vermont.gov

- Virginia Dept. of Social Services:
  www.dss.state.va.us

- Washington Dept. of Social & health Services:
  www.dshs.wa.gov

- West Virginia Dept. of Health & Human Resources:
  www.dhhr.wv.gov

- Wisconsin Dept. of Health & Family Services:
  www.dhs.wisconsin.gov

- Wyoming Dept. of Health:
  www.health.wyo.gov/aging

## Business Insurance

Business insurance provides financial protection for your new senior home care business. When you are providing home care services in client's homes, almost anything can, and will, happen, but you can make sure any potential liability is covered by an insurance umbrella.

Working with an insurance broker is usually advised, as they can provide quotes from several companies for the different types of insurance you will need. One broker that specializes in home care businesses is the Solutions Group, online at: www.homehealthins.com.

Here's what is recommended for most home care businesses:

**Commercial Crime Bond.** If an employee steals from a client's home (or yours), you are covered. Theft is the most common claim in home care, and often includes theft of cash, jewelry, drugs or unauthorized use of a client's credit card.

**General Liability.** This type of insurance covers damage to a client's property, libel and slander, slip and fall claims and other risks.

**Non-Owned Auto Liability.** If an employee causes an at-fault accident while driving on the job, you're covered. For example, a caregiver is driving a client to a doctor's appointment and hits a pedestrian.

**Professional Liability.** For a home care service, this insurance covers damages from improper care or absence of proper care. For example, a fall while assisting a client up the stairs, or a fall because the caregiver was not helping the client down the stairs while on duty.

**Workmen's Compensation.** This insurance is mandatory in 49 states and covers on-the-job injuries. This insurance protects employers from lawsuits caused by workplace accidents and provides compensation for lost income and medical care to employees injured in workplace accidents or caused by work related illnesses.

Most states have a government sponsored plan, which is usually cheaper than private workman's compensation insurance. If your state does not, always get at least two quotes for this insurance.

When you're getting started, you will be asked to estimate your payroll to determine the insurance premium. It is generally best to use a low estimate until you have actual numbers, as your initial deposit is based on the estimate.

While you may have heard it's best to classify your employees as "independent contractors" to avoid workman's compensation insurance, don't do it unless they have an actual business license and insurance.

The I.R.S. and the courts have tough standards for determining whether a person is an employee or an independent contractor. The courts call it the "right to control" test. If the hiring person controls the way the work is carried out, such as hours worked or which client to visit, the relationship between the parties is employer/employee. An additional test: if a person depends on a business for steady income, they are an employee. If the employer has no authority over how a person does their work, that person could be classified as an independent contractor.

## Taxes & Accounting

There are three types of taxes you'll be responsible for as a business owner, employment taxes, income tax and self-employment tax. If you do not have employees, you generally do not have to pay employment taxes, but just a self-employment tax.

 It's a good idea to visit a tax pro, such as an accountant, to learn just what taxes will be required for the type of business you plan to start. They can also advise you what information they will require to help you at tax time, such as a profit and loss statement.

To keep accounting costs low, you should do as much as possible yourself. Today, most accounting software for small businesses has gone online, and is called "cloud" software, as it is web-hosted rather than from a program installed on your computer. This allows the software company to easily update programs to reflect changes in tax laws and other regulations.

A small senior home care business does not need a high-powered, expensive accounting system, but something that is simple enough to be easy to understand and use. It should also be capable of generating invoices for your clients, and reports needed by your accountant or tax professional.

As I write this, there are over a dozen capable accounting software programs that are suitable for your small business. They all have the basic capabilities covered, so it's up to you to choose the best fit for you. Here are my current favorites:

**Fresh Books.** This cloud-based accounting program is considered one of the best invoicing solutions available, which is important for any senior service business with dozens of clients to bill regularly. It even includes time-tracking, so you can easily add billable time to an invoice. You can also add auto-billing and automatic payment reminders and thank you notes!

Like most, they offer a free trial period so new users can see if they like the program before spending any money. Their pricing is based on the number of clients you invoice. Because it is web-based, there are no downloads or installations, and it is compatible with all operating systems as long as you have internet access.

Fresh Books is very easy to use, a big plus for a non-accountant like me (and you?) The setup is simple and quick, and the interface is easy to figure out and logical. Help is available online and by phone. When I last called, the wait time was under 2 minutes.

**GoDaddy Bookkeeping.** This software, formerly called Outright, is more user-friendly than most accounting programs. It's more of a bookkeeping program aimed at small businesses that just need to account for income, expenses and taxes.

The company was started by two guys who worked at Intuit, the parent company of Quickbooks, to offer a simpler solution for small business owners who didn't know much about accounting but needed to have accurate data for their taxes.

This software is also cloud-based, so there are no downloads, and you can access your account anywhere you have an internet connection, even on your iPad or smartphone. There is a free plan if you just need to track income and expenses, and a paid version which is quite affordable – currently about $120 per year.

Like all the other cloud accounting programs, you can link your accounts, such as bank accounts, credit cards, PayPal and even your eBay seller account. Then it automatically downloads the information daily. Of course, it can create and send invoices to customers, and has a great built-in time sheet, so you can track billable hours to a specific client and send an invoice based on those hours.

Unlike most of the other online programs, there is no extra charge for additional clients. Whether you have two clients or two hundred the cost is the same – currently about $10 a month for the paid version. To learn more, visit: www.bookkeeping. godaddy.com

**QuickBooks Online.** Everyone has heard of Quicken, which has been available since the mid-80s, followed by QuickBooks. It is the Big Dog of accounting software and used by thousands of companies.

QuickBooks Online has a 3-tier pricing plan, and a 30-day free trial. The basic "Simple Start" plan includes invoicing and estimates, as well as all the normal accounting features. The "Essentials" plan adds an accounts payable function to track and pay bills. The "Plus" plan allows subscribers to track inventory and generate 1099 forms.

The software is web-hosted, so no downloads or installation is required, and is compatible with Windows and Mac OS X operating systems. Setup is easy and quick and includes several how-to videos. There are a huge numbers of features available to users, but the less-used ones are kept in the background for regular users.

Because it is more complex than the other programs I've mentioned, there are a few challenges, and a steeper learning curve. For example, when you send an invoice, it automatically includes a "Pay Now" button, which requires you to use the Quicken electronic payment system. Guess what? That system is more costly than other options, such as PayPal.

Another problem is poor support. Long wait times for phone support are common, and online support is spotty. This could improve however, so check a few online reviews before signing on with them. Do a web search for "QuickBooks online community forum" to find out what others currently think.

## Business Plan

Although many business experts insist that a business plan is essential to starting a small business, that's not always true. For every business that fails because of poor planning, there are five that never succeed because of too much planning. As the great Michael Jordan said, "Just do it!"

The secret of a successful senior home care business is providing the services that people want to buy. A business plan can't tell you that, but real customers can. Instead of wasting a lot of time and energy coming up with a business plan, just start talking to your potential customers to find out what they need and figure out how to give it to them.

Regardless of how much planning you do, it's only a hunch - an educated guess about how well your business will do. The danger is, by spending too much time on planning, you'll have less energy/time/money to try new marketing ideas. The secret is to test your ideas as quickly and cheaply as possible, then improve and refine them.

And speaking of cheap & quick, here's a way to do a very simple business plan for your new senior home care business. If you plan to borrow money from a relative or friend - the most common source of funding for small startup businesses - do an "executive summary" business plan to show them you've done your homework. It should cover just the business plan basics, with an overview of the business, a market analysis with a look at your competition, and an estimate of your first year's sales. It assumes that you will not have employees or buying or leasing property or equipment. Here's a sample:

## DEPENDABLE SENIOR HOME CARE BUSINESS PLAN

**Business Overview:** Dependable Senior Home Care is a new in-home care service based in Bend, Oregon, specializing in senior care. The business will cover the greater Bend area. Our customers are seniors who need non-medical care to remain in their own home.

**Market Analysis:** The demand for reliable, cost-effective home care services has been growing in the area for several years as the town's senior population continues to grow. There are only two other local senior care services in the area, and we believe there is ample room, due to our growing senior population, for another reliable senior in-home care service.

**Marketing Strategy:** The marketing strategy of Dependable Senior Home Care is to provide dependable and exceptional services to seniors and their out-of-town children who have a regular need for home care services. This will ensure that the business will have a regular, steady income from repeat customers. The second part of our marketing strategy will be to gain customers who need home care services occasionally, such as anyone recovering from an illness or surgery, or those who are unable to leave home for other medical reasons.

**First Year Goal:** Based on the size of the local senior care market and the fact that Dependable Senior Home Care will be a one-person business, our sales projection for the first year is $60,000. We plan to build our customer base through direct contact with prospective customers and word-of-mouth referrals from happy customers to continue to grow our service and add employees as demand grows.

## Free help to start your new business

There is a free resource available to start-up companies, including senior care businesses. SCORE is a government program that taps the experience and brainpower of retired business owners to help new owners get off to a successful start. If you find you need a comprehensive business plan to get funding for your new courier business, SCORE can help you with that as well. To find the nearest office, visit: www.score.org.

## Senior Home Care Business Forms

Once you have picked a business name and checked to make sure no one else has claimed the name, you can print your business cards, flyers and forms. Check with local suppliers, such as your favorite office supply store, or online printers, like www.gotprint. net, www.psprint.com,www.uprinting.com and www.vistaprint. com. In chapter 5, you'll find all the basic forms to use, including:

- **Service Agreement.** This agreement spells out the working relationship between you and your client, which may be the person you are caring for, or a responsible person, such as their son or daughter. To prevent any misunderstanding, this agreement spells out the service you will be providing, the hourly rate, any surcharges for weekend or holiday hours, mileage charges, length of service and a weekly schedule.

- **Care Recipient Information Sheet.** This form should be filled out with the help of either the senior you are caring for, or the person who is responsible for their care. It includes emergency contact information, physician contact information, any known allergies or diet restrictions, and a clear explanation of the medical conditions of the care recipient.

- **Assessment Form.** Each new client is unique, and you'll need to sit down with each prospective client or a family member, to determine their physical and mental capacities and which services might be appropriate for them.

The first meeting takes about an hour to complete. In addition to filling out the assessment form, this is a good time for you, as a potential service provider, to establish trust and confidence. Be sure to mention any special skills or qualifications you have that would make you more able to service their needs.

Make an appointment with your prospect and call the day before to confirm the appointment. Bring a service agreement and a plan of care form along so you are prepared to sign up the prospect at the end of the meeting.

Don't forget that, at this first meeting, you are an unknown, so smile and be positive about what you can do to help the client. Do your best to remember the client's first name and the names of their family members, then use their first names often during the meeting. In addition, be patient and understanding. Also be sure to ask permission before starting the assessment: "Would you mind if I asked you a few questions now?"

## Plan of Care Form

When you have completed the assessment form, it's time to recommend a care plan. Always be positive, and suggest areas where the client needs assistance, such as personal care, transportation or companionship. If the client or a family member agree, check the box next to that item, then discuss the next care option, until the entire plan of care form is complete. Finally, discuss how many hours per day and days per week would be required or recommended.

At this point in your client interview, you'll need to discuss hourly rates for the services you recommend. If the client's budget is limited, ask "What would work for you." For example, if you feel five days a week would be best, but the client can't afford that, suggest two or three days a week. It's important to find a solution that works for both you and your client.

Once you've reached agreement on the services, hours and rates, fill out the service agreement and have your client sign it, then collect the deposit.

You'll find all these forms, plus a new prospect form, in chapter 5.

## Spy for A Day?

One of the most important tasks in setting up your new senior home care business is to find out what similar businesses are doing in your area. If you live in a larger city, it will be easy to find other senior care businesses. If you're in a small town, talk to senior home care businesses in the closest large town or city. Don't just talk to one ... call at least three.

To learn what you need to know, you must become a "spy for a day." Call other senior home care providers and pretend to be a adult child of an elderly parent who may need help. Here are the questions you need to ask:

1. What kind of services can you provide for my "dad/mom?"

2. How long have you been in business.

3. What are your rates?

4. Do you require a deposit?

5. Are your caregivers bonded and insured?

6. Who is your insurance company for liability? (This is important, as home care liability insurance is a specialized

niche and finding an insurance company that covers caregivers can be a challenge.)

7.  What happens if dad/mom doesn't like their caregiver?

8.  If we are not happy with your services, how much notice is required to cancel?

9.  How often do you bill us & do you accept credit cards?

## Record Keeping

To make it easy to find and store your client records and other business paperwork, you'll need a 2 or 4 drawer lockable file cabinet. You can find affordable file cabinets at Walmart, Target, or office supply stores, or buy used for even more savings.

Keeping information about your clients confidential and secure is a legal requirement, so store all your client forms, such as service agreements, care recipient information sheets, assessment forms and plan of care forms in a lockable file cabinet in a secure place.

One simple system that works well for a senior home care business is to create a separate file for each client. It's helpful to color code the file folders so you can easily identify current or past clients – green for current and red for past – for example.

In chapter five, you'll find the forms you'll need for your new senior home care business. To customize the forms with your contact information, scan the forms and have them turned into custom forms. Here's how:

Go to www.fiverr.com and do a search for "fillable forms." For just a few dollars, one of the sellers there can turn any form, together with your business name and contact information, at the top, into professional forms. Once that's done, you can make as many copies as you need for your new senior home care business.

You can then copy the forms at any copy shop. A multi-function copier/printer at your office is a real time saver, as you can make copies as needed. In addition, you can print other documents, such as invoices, directly from your computer, or fax a document.

My favorite brand is Brother, which offers several affordable models. Do a search at Amazon.com for "Brother multi-function printer." for discounted prices. I suggest a laser printer instead of an ink-jet printer, as a laser printer is much less expensive to operate than an ink-jet printer, and cheaper to buy.

## Run your senior home care business with just a phone

Just a few years ago, smartphones did not exist. Today, a smartphone packs far more computing power than the computers used to put a man on the moon! Now almost everything you need to run your senior home care service – from scheduling to billing to getting paid on the go – can be done from your smartphone or tablet.

Running a small service business means that you must wear many hats. You are the CEO (Chief Everything Officer) of your business, so whatever needs to get done falls right on your shoulders.

Fortunately for you, there's an app for everything you need to get done, and it's available free or for a very low cost at the app store. Using the right apps can help you deliver great customer service, keep a tight and profitable schedule and win the hearts of your customers.

As your senior home care business grows, you'll need to keep track of customer schedules days in advance, keep track of each customer's special needs, and make sure you get paid by your private pay customers, whether they have cash or a credit card.

To help you do all that with the most productivity and the least hassle, let's take a look at the best apps for your senior home care service.

## Scheduling your jobs

A great calendar is almost as good as having your own personal assistant to help keep your days flowing smoothly so you can make more money. Without a calendar app on your smartphone, you might forget appointments and have unhappy customers.

Since your smartphone already comes with a built-in calendar app, so why not use that one? Simply because there are other alternative calendar apps that do a better job, especially for this specific business.

They are fast and easy to use, so you don't waste time searching for what you need. The best apps have a simple, uncluttered look, so checking it several times a day will be a pleasant experience, not a frustrating one.

The two most widely used calendar apps that are pre-installed on either any Android phone or the iPhone are Google Calendar and Apple Calendar. Both have a lot going for them, including the ability to connect to your calendar across multiple devices, like your computer, tablet or smartphone.

Google Calendar allows you to keep several calendars, so you can separate personal and work schedules, and allows you to color-code entries to make it easy to find a specific item. You can also use it to search your contact file or Gmail account.

Apple Calendar is built into every iPhone, and syncs with all other Apple devices. The clean and simple design makes it easier to use than Google Calendar. For example, tapping the + sign creates a new event, like a new customer and their schedule.

Now let's take a look at the other calendar apps that might be better for you. My personal favorite for iPhone users is Fantastical 2, by Flexbits. It's incredibly easy to use, fast and powerful. When you look at your day's events, they are all readable and easy to understand. You can add new events with just a few taps, and even view your schedule in 3 modes to allow you to view days, weeks or months. The cost is around $5 at the Apple app store.

If you have an Android phone, my favorite choice for upgrading is called Business Calendar, by Appgenix software. The interface is simply amazing – you almost feel it was custom designed just for your business.

Instead of having fixed views for a day or a week, you simply tap and drag the days you want to see, such as Tuesday through Friday of next week. Tapping on a specific day brings up a pop-up of that day's events. You can drag and drop events, so if your client needs a home visit four days a week, which most do, you can easily add that event on multiple days in just a minute.

Plus, it's very easy to use, and much easier to navigate than almost any other calendar app out there. The cost is about $5 at the Google Play store.

## Managing Your Contacts

As your senior home care business grows, your customer list will grow as well, and you must have a way to manage that list, so you can keep track of your customers and any special needs they may have. Fortunately, there are two great apps available to just that for you.

If you have an Android phone, Contacts + is a must-have app. With over 10 million users, you know it's got to be great. What I like best is the built-in spam blocker, so you don't have to deal with spammers. In addition, Contacts+ includes a backup service for your contacts, so if you switch or lose your phone, your contacts are always available.

If you have an iPhone, my choice is called Simpler Contacts, which of course keeps things simple but still has the features to make it useful. Plus, it's very easy to learn and use. One of my favorite features allows you to send the same text message or email to a group of people.

For example, if you plan a vacation in 3 weeks, you can message or email your entire customer list to let them know. If you're having a special promotion, like a discount on new services, send it out as well. You can back up your contacts using Google Drive or Dropbox. Simpler Contacts is available at the Apple app store.

## How to get paid on the go

Countries around the world are moving towards alternative payments and away from cash, such as the wildly popular app, WePay, in China, which requires just a swipe of your smartphone. That's a hot trend in the U.S. and Canada as well, with cash-free services like Apple Pay and Venmo growing in popularity every day.

To handle the growing number of customers who prefer not to use cash, you'll need to provide a method for them to use a credit card easily. Fortunately, there are several companies that offer mobile payment processing for small businesses like yours. Three that stand out for affordability and ease of use are Square, SparkPay and Propay.

**Square** is a user-friendly payment system for accepting credit and debit cards. Square's mobile card reader, which plugs into your smart phone, is free when you sign up. Square works with both Android and Apple smartphones and tablets. They currently charge a flat 2.75% processing fee. www.square.com.

**SparkPay** is part of CapitalOne, the well-known credit card company, and provides a solid mobile payment system. You can start with their "Go" plan, which charges 2.65% per transaction, then switch to the "Pro" plan, when your volume hits $2,000 per month. With that volume, the fee falls to 1.99% per transaction. Users also report the customer phone support is better than Square, an important consideration. SparkPay.com.

Finally, **ProPay**, a service that has been around for years, offers all the features needed for mobile payment processing, including a mobile card reader, and rates as low as 2.40% for processing transactions. ProPay.com.

CHAPTER THREE

# Finding Customers

Without new customers, your new senior home care business will never thrive and make a profit. Marketing is an essential part of starting and growing your new business, and this chapter will give you the tools to find all the customers you want, with very little expense.

Small business owners today have far more marketing options available to them than just a few years ago. Now, because of the explosive growth of the internet as an advertising medium, many of the most effective marketing tools are free or close to it.

In additional to internet-based marketing, there are also dozens of traditional marketing methods available for any business owner that takes the time to use them. Almost all are free or almost free.

From flyers to publicity releases, smart small business owners have been using these proven methods to boost sales and profits for many years, but now, thanks to the internet, your marketing message can reach more people for less money than ever before.

I'll go over dozens of free and low-cost marketing ideas for your new business in this chapter. You don't have to use all of them - just experiment with several to see which one's work best for your business. Whether you're launching a new business or growing an existing business, free marketing can help you grow your business without spending a lot to do so.

The material we'll cover in this chapter is meant to be an idea generator for you, so skim the content, and pick the ideas that interest you. I'm sure you will find the perfect combination of ideas to boost your sales and profits for years to come.

**Never forget the Golden Rule of marketing - treat your customers and prospects as you would want to be treated, and they will be loyal customers for life!**

Capable and dependable senior in-home caregivers are hard to find. If they are good at what they do – providing high-quality care to seniors – they will always be in demand and working as much as they choose. Once you've had a few clients to give you 5-star recommendations, you can expect to be busy.

But when you are just starting out, you do not have a track record or a stellar reputation in the senior community, so you will need to advertise in order to get your first clients. Here are the 4 best ways to find clients:

1. **Free Ads.**   Don't waste your money on newspaper ads – there are plenty of ways to advertise for free. Many caregivers have found a simple ad, repeated regularly on Craigslist.org can bring in a steady supply of new prospects. Here is a sample ad you can adapt for your own use:

   **Senior Care in Your Home**

   **Call Today for Help Today**
   - ✓ *Caring Companionship*
   - ✓ *Respite Care*

- ✓ *Errands and Appointments*
- ✓ *Help with Personal Care*
- ✓ *Meal Preparation*
- ✓ *Light Housekeeping*

**Free Consultation – Licensed, Bonded, Insured**
**Your Business Name & Phone number**

2. **Local Referrals.** Those who work with seniors regularly are the best source of referrals for your senior care business. Here's who to contact:

   **Attorneys** who specialize in elder law can be an excellent source of clients, as they often contacted when a senior has significant life changes.

   *Assisted Living Facilities.* When seniors return home after a stay in an assisted living facility, they often need in-home care.

   **Churches**. Pastors, ministers and rabbis deal regularly with the old and sick and are often aware when they need assistance at home. Leave your business card and a few flyers with each pastor you contact.

   **Hospice**. When a senior has only a few months to live, a home caregiver can improve their quality of life during those final months. Contact your local hospice to find out how you can help.

   **Hospitals**. Most hospitals have a discharge planner or a social worker on staff, who is in a position to recommend a home care provider.

**Other senior care providers**. Often a home care provider can be too busy or understaffed to take on any new clients. Introduce yourself to other care providers in your community to tap into this referral network.

**Word of mouth.** Satisfied clients are the best advertisement, and far more credible than any other form of advertising. Often one happy client will recommend you to several friends, who may also become clients. Be sure to leave a few business cards with clients to pass along.

Don't forget – you create satisfied clients when you provide quality service, charge fair prices and always practice the Golden Rule – ***Treat Others as You Would Want to be Treated.***

3. **Online Referrals.** Many seniors, as well as the adult children of seniors, now use the Internet to find a senior care provider. Even if you have your own website, you may want to register with the online care provider referral services. Here are a few to consider:

   1. www.eldercarelink.com

   2. www.actikare.com

   3. Caring from a Distance. www.cfad.org

   4. www.caring.com

   5. www.carepathways.com

   6. www.caregiver.org

Many states now maintain an online registry of home care providers. This can be a good source of referrals for your new home care business. To find out if your state has a registry, do a web search for "your state" home care registry.

## The Best Free Advertising

Satisfied clients are a small business "secret weapon," as they are usually repeat/regular clients and they tell their friends about your business, yet your out-of-pocket advertising cost is zero. Word-of-mouth can be your most effective advertising if you provide a service that is so good your clients are loyal for years. Here are two ways to encourage your happy clients to share their enthusiasm about your business:

Always give your clients more than what they expect. Zappo's does it with free shipping and 110% customer service, bakers do it with the "baker's dozen" of an extra roll or pastry. Think about how you might surprise your clients when they choose you to help them with their needs.

Ask for word-of-mouth by asking satisfied clients to refer their friends to you. You can even "bribe" them with a discount or gift if their friend mentions their name when they buy.

Always treat your satisfied clients with loyalty, kindness and consideration (Just like you want to be treated!) The more satisfied clients you have, the more additional satisfied clients you'll gain. Like a snowball rolling downhill, it's a growing circle of boosters that gets bigger every day along with your profits.

### A Smile is Still the Best Free Advertising

A simple smile is rarely mentioned in advertising textbooks or classes, but it is one of the most important marketing tools we all possess. A smile forms a powerful human bond and shows you regard a person as a human being, not just another customer or business prospect.

A smile makes a person feel good, and perhaps even feel you are a friend. As you know, folks like to buy from friends. Ask yourself how you felt the last time someone smiled at you. How did it make you feel? I thought so. Remember, smiles are free, requiring only a small amount of energy. Don't forget that a smile works when you're chatting on the phone, as the person on the other end can actually feel the smile.

Business success is all about paying attention to the little details, like a genuine smile. Share yours with every customer and prospect you meet and let it work its magic for you.

## Customer Service

Marketing pros rank customer service right up there in the top three success factors for small business. In these competitive times, running a customer- focused business can make the difference between success and failure. Like most of the ideas in this chapter, customer service costs almost nothing out- of- pocket.

Frank Cooper, the author of "The Customer Signs Your Paycheck," has a checklist for business owners called:

## The 10 Commandments of Customer Relations

1.  The customer is never an interruption to your work. The customer is your real reason for being in business. Chores can wait.

2. Greet every customer with a friendly smile. Customers are people, and they like friendly contact. They usually return it.

3. Call customers by name. Make a game of learning customers' names. See how many you can remember. This is a valuable habit.

4. Remember--you are the company!

5. Never argue with a customer. The customer is always right (in his own eyes). Be a good listener, agree with him where you can, and then do what you can to make him happy.

6. Never say, "I don't know." If you don't know the answer to a customer's question, say, "That's a good question. Let me find out for you."

7. Remember that the customer pays your wages. Every dollar you earn comes from the customer's pocket. Treat him like the boss. He signs your paycheck.

8. State things in a positive way. Choose positive words when speaking to a customer. It takes practice, but it is a valuable habit that will help you become an effective communicator.

9. Brighten every customer's day! Make it a point to do something that brings a little sunshine into each customer's life, and soon you'll discover that your own life is happier and brighter!

10. Go the extra mile! Always do just a little more than the customer expects you to do. You will be richly rewarded for this habit!

## Make Money with Reminders

Your existing customers are like money in the bank. They know you; they trust you and are far more likely to purchase from you than someone who is not yet a client. One of the easiest ways for a business to make money is to contact past customers with a special offer.

For example, send out an e-mail coupon to your client and prospect mailing list every month. The coupon could be for specials, like a 10% discount for a new customer, or a non- specific offer, like 20% off when a customer tries a new service.

Everyone loves to be remembered, so think about sending out birthday cards or personalized reminders. For some ideas, visit www.sendoutcards.com. An old-fashioned handwritten note is still an effective tool. Very few businesses take the time to do this, which makes it even more effective.

For example, drop a thank-you note in the mail to each customer two or three times a year. Nothing fancy, just let them know you appreciate them and value their business.

The simple act of communicating regularly is a powerful business builder when practiced often and sincerely. Take a few minutes every week to stay in touch with your customers, and you'll be well rewarded.

## Let Google Help Your Customers Find You

If your business depends on local customers, you'll enjoy a free listing in Google Places. Today, most of your customers are using internet search engines to find local services and businesses instead of the traditional Yellow Pages. So it makes sense to take advantage of these free listings offered by online directories for businesses. The most popular, and currently the largest, of all is Google Places.

You can start by visiting http://places.google.com and clicking on the 'get started now' button under 'Get your business found on Google.' After signing in, or signing up, at no cost, you'll be able to list your business. You can include photos or add photos or a map.

Getting a basic listing is simple, but there are a few ways to help your business appear near the top of the listings if you have any local competitors listed.

First, remember Google values good content, so be sure you fill out your business profile with quality information. Follow their directions for completing the listing to the letter and don't leave any blank spaces.

Next, encourage your customers to leave feedback and positive reviews on any web sites related to your business, such as local directories published by groups like the Chamber of Commerce. You can also ask customers to leave reviews or testimonials on your own website but be sure they are legitimate and genuine.

Last, if you don't have one yet, your business needs a website, ideally with its own domain name. Having a website will give your business, however small it is, a giant boost in the Google rankings.

As more and more businesses sign up for Google Places, those who have a website will have a better shot at a listing near the top. Almost any web hosting service, such as SiteGround, mentioned earlier, can help you get a domain name and set up a Wordpress site, which ranks well with Google, as Wordpress is easy to index.

Besides Google Places, other major online 'local' directories worth exploring are:

http://bing.com/local

http://listings.local.yahoo.com

http://listings.local.yahoo.com

http://yelp.com

http://linkedin.com

http://citysearch.com

http://listings.mapquest.com

http://advertise.local.com

http://angieslist.com

## Local S.E.O.

Since your new senior transportation business will depend on local customers, you must use location- based keywords, such as "NEMT business- your town." The reason local SEO is so important for your business is because almost half of all Google searches are searching for a local business.

For example, the fastest growing search term on Google is "near me" as in "Italian restaurant near me." Since Google and other search engines can easily determine your approximate location, this enables them to deliver the results you are searching for with high accuracy.

To make it even easier for you to find what you're looking for, Google provides a "Map Pack," a set of 3 high ranking local businesses, complete with a map of their locations from Google maps. Underneath the Map Pack, you'll find the rest of the results for your search.

## How to find the best keywords for local S.E.O.

Do a Google search for words and phrases that relate to your business, one at a time, and make a list of them. For example, "senior home care service near me," "home care my town." When you enter your search term, you'll see a list of additional search terms. Take a close look at those to see if any are suitable for your business. Save your list of search terms to use when setting up your "Google My Business" profile.

## How to set up your Google My Business profile

Google My Business (www.google.com/business) is the number one factor Google uses to rank your business in local searches. When setting up your profile, be sure to include your full business name, address, and phone number (NAP). Google uses this information to ensure that your business is legitimate. Also, the NAP on your website should be an exact match for your Google My Business listing.

If it's not a match, Google may rank your business lower in local searches. Even spelling counts here - if your business address is 123 Lincoln Avenue, makes sure it's "Avenue" and not "Ave." so the Google search engine doesn't get confused.

When filling out your profile on GMB, choose a broad category that best describes your business - "senior home care" for example.

Also fill out the "services" tab in your profile that describes what your business does.

## Google Reviews

Reviews are another major ranking factor in the Google ranking system. You may have noticed that business with many reviews, especially positive reviews, always ranks higher than those with no reviews. That's why you'll want to get as many positive reviews as you can as soon as you can.

When you get a review, good, bad or lukewarm, reply to it inside the Google My Business dashboard. That shows you care and is also a factor in Google rankings. It doesn't have to be a long reply to be effective. For example, "Thanks for the 5-star review. We really appreciate your business," or "Thanks for the feedback."

## How to Get More Google Reviews

Keep in mind that most customers won't bother to leave a review, even if they love your service, unless asked. It's easy to do. In fact, Google makes it easy for both you and your customers.

Go to your GMB account dashboard and locate the "get more reviews" card. There, you can get a link to your review page that you can copy and paste into an email to send to your customers.

Apply all these simple SEO tips, and soon your new business will show up on page 1 of Google search results. All without having to spend any money. Don't put this off any longer than necessary, as it's one of the best "free lunches" you'll ever receive!

## Social Media Marketing

**Facebook** is the largest social media network in the world, with over 2 billion active users. Most users are between the ages of 25 and 65, but the over-65 users are the fastest growing group! That's great news, as these are the people you want to reach about your home watch business.

Because of its size and the large number of users, Facebook is the best social media to get your new business shared and discovered by both new prospects and your current clients. That's why it is often called "the largest word-of-mouth marketing resource on the planet."

Facebook can also be the biggest time waster if you let it, as it's easy to linger there for hours. But you have a business to build and grow, so let's focus on doing just that, with some help from Facebook, in less than 15 minutes a day.

**First rule -** Don't waste your money on Facebook ads. No one visits Facebook to look for services or products. They visit to see what their friends are doing. With that in mind, here's how to get started without spending a dime.

It's important to note that you must create a Facebook page, not a personal profile, also called a Personal Timeline. They do not permit personal profiles for commercial use, so if you are already a Facebook user you must create a separate page for your home watch business.

You can create a Facebook Page by searching "create a page" in the searcher at the top of the page, or by clicking the "create a page" button at the top of any Facebook page.

Before you create your new Facebook page, spend some time thinking about the page name you will use. Ideally, it should be short, easy to remember, promise a benefit, and describe your business.

In the "About" section of your new Facebook Page, include as much information about your business as possible, so current clients and prospects can find all your important information in one page.

You can also optimize your page by choosing one of the pre-made templates. The Professional Services template is a good fit for most senior home care businesses. You'll find the templates under: Settings>Edit Page.

Next, create an eye-catching cover photo for your Facebook page. Look at other senior home care businesses, both on Facebook and by doing a web search for "senior home care business" to see what others have done.

Ideally, your cover photo should communicate what your business is all about, so take the time to do it right. The easiest way to get a good cover photo designed is to hire a designer at Fiverr.com.

It will cost you around $5 to $15, but it's money well spent. Just enter "design Facebook cover" in the Fiverr.com search bar to locate dozens of capable designers. Be sure to mention that you want the image size to be 820 X 312 pixels per Facebook guidelines.

When you've uploaded your new cover photo, click it to add a text description. Describe your business in a positive way and, if possible, encourage viewers to click on the cover photo to get more "likes."

You'll also want to add a Facebook profile photo in a 180 x 180-pixel size. Remember, this profile photo appears in a follower's news feeds, in comment replies, and all over Facebook, so use a great photo. (Don't forget to smile!)

Once you've set up your Facebook page, stay active with regular posts. Most pros find 3X a week works well yet doesn't require a lot of time.

Don't forget to post about special experiences you've had with clients that others might enjoy. Share the story and a picture or two of you and your client in a post.

## Is a Facebook Page Better Than a Web Site?

Yes, and no. You can set up a Facebook page in about an hour and it's free. That page allows you to stay in touch with clients and prospects and build relationships. If a Facebook page is not working for you delete it or ignore it. Keeping your Facebook page up to date with your current information, such as rates and services offered, is quick and easy.

But - you are not in control. Facebook is in control and can change or restrict what you can do on the site overnight. In addition, anyone can post negative comments or complaints on your page if they wish.

If you create a website, you're in control. You own it. You get to decide what it looks like and what it contains. You can have hundreds of pages or posts or just a simple one-pager.

Consumers today expect a business to have a website. They trust a business more when they see a "real" website. Also, having your own website allows you to post all your service information at the site, like the services you provide, monthly specials, testimonials and more.

My choice would be to have both a Facebook page and a website. You have the best of both worlds - and you don't have to say "follow me on Facebook."

**Twitter** can be a powerful social media tool for your business that can help you educate clients about your services, reach new prospects for your business and connect you to other Twitter users with similar interests.

Here are just two of the many ways Twitter can help your business:

- ✓ Drive traffic to your website. Unlike other social media, you can re-use content from your website or other original material repeatedly. Your tweets can include your website URL, text, images, even a video.

- ✓ Google indexes your twitter bio and tweets, which helps you get found by search engines. Make sure your bio contains the keywords you want Google to find and index, such as your business name and what your business does. Be sure to tweet regularly so you increase the odds of ranking higher in Google Search.

Last, use hashtags (#) to get more attention for your tweets, show your support and help people who don't know you to follow you. To learn what topics are hot or trending up right now, check Twitter Trends or hashtagify.me.

It's free and easy to make an account - just visit twitter.com, enter your name, phone and email address and create a password for your new account. After you've signed up, you can add more information for your account.

Next it's time to pick your Twitter "handle," which is the same as a username. The best handle is your business name, if it is available. You can check all the social networks for name availability at knowem.com.

If your handle/name is not available, you can add HQ to your company name, add a "get" in front of your name, or add your location, such as your town's name, to your handle.

Whatever handle you choose, make sure it is as short as possible, because you only have 280 characters to use, and they count your username in that 280 words when someone responds to your messages.

**LinkedIn** is a place for companies and individuals to connect on a professional, not personal, level. Unlike other social media sites, folks who join LinkedIn are not joining for enjoyment and fun but to access new business opportunities and connections.

As the owner of a small business, you can use LinkedIn to connect to other related service businesses, promote your own business and build relationships with other professionals that have common interests.

Getting started is no more difficult than at other social networks. You start by creating your own personal account and profile. A LinkedIn profile is much more professional You won't find funny cat videos or cute baby photos.

Keep that in mind when creating your profile. In your profile, be sure to include your best work-related qualities so others will see the advantages of working with you.

Although you can upgrade to several higher levels of paid subscriptions, the basic account should be fine for almost all small businesses. Your basic profile can include a summary of yourself, contact information, links to your blog or website or other social media pages, like Facebook, and what you're doing now professionally.

Once you've completed your personal profile and published it, you can:

1. Look for connections - people you know or would like to know.

2. Join a group of other users who share common interests.

3. Have an online "business card" where potential clients can learn about and connect with you.

4. Boost your online reputation as a senior transportation professional.

There are hundreds of other social media sites, as you may have noticed when you visited knowem.com. but most are useful only for entertainment, not helping you grow your house watch business. These three, Facebook, Twitter and LinkedIn will help you stay connected, expand your network, and increase your profits.

## Stay in Touch with a Free Newsletter

One of the best and least expensive ways to stay in touch with your clients and potential clients is by sending them an e-mail newsletter. By using an email, the big expenses of a traditional newsletter, printing and postage, are eliminated. Your newsletter should do two things:

1. Pass along useful information your customers are happy to read, even forward to their friends.

2. Increase your profits by either helping sell more of your services or attract more prospects who will buy from you.

3. The easiest way to make sure your newsletter accomplishes those two goals is to just ask your clients and prospects what they want before you send out the first issue and keep asking them what they want in the newsletter. How often should a newsletter be sent to clients? Most experts say it's not how often that matters, but the quality of the content.

   Some prefer a frequent schedule, such as every two weeks or once a month, while others may only do a quarterly newsletter. If you have built a list of loyal clients, they don't really care how often they receive an issue.

Be sure to ask a favor at the end of each newsletter: *"If you've enjoyed this newsletter, please forward it to your friends."* Doing so will grow your subscriber list and your profits over time.

When your e-mail list has grown beyond a few subscribers, it's time to get some professional help. My favorites are www.MailChimp.com and www.mailerlite.com

At Mail Chimp, for free, you'll have access to professionally designed message templates and sign-up forms, and up to 2,000 customers or 12,000 emails a month and compliance with all anti-spam regulations.

You'll love the free service, plus the freedom from tedious mailing list maintenance. Another excellent provider with free service for up to 1,000 subscribers is mailerlite.com.

## Ten Tips for a Successful E-Mail Newsletter

According to the e-mail pros, a well-done e-mail newsletter can produce $40 in profits for every dollar you spend. That's a powerful incentive to spend the time on staying in touch with your customers and prospects with e-mails. Here are ten tips that will help you make more money and build customer loyalty with your own e-mail newsletter.

1. Current content. Be sure to date each newsletter issue when you send it out so readers will know the content is current.

2. You don't have to be a writer to produce an e-mail newsletter that gets results. Just write as you speak and focus on the topic you want to communicate with your clients.

3. Your newsletter need not look professional to succeed. Just a simple text message will work just fine. That said, most of the professional e-mail list management services, like www.MailerLite.com.com and www.MailChimp.com offer free HTML templates that can dress up your message.

4. The best ideas for content in your e-mail newsletter will come from your readers. Ask them often about what they would like to see covered in future issues.

5. Keep your newsletter short. If you have several ideas to share, break them up into individual newsletter issues, or include an excerpt, with a link to the full text at your web site or blog.

6. Try not to go too long between issues - two weeks to a month is a reasonable interval to aim for.

7. The cyber-gremlins will always try to mess with your e-mails, so get used to it. E-mails get lost, trapped in reader's spam filters, or just plain disappear. Subscribers will forget they subscribed and accuse you of spamming them or click the spam button instead of unsubscribing. Just view it all as a part of your learning curve and stay calm. Using one of the services mentioned in #3 can help minimize problems, and the cost is reasonable. In fact, as I write this, Mail Chimp and MailerLite offer a free service if you have a small (1,000 to 2,000 subscribers) list.

8. Keep your sales pitches under control. While folks expect you to sell them something, they get upset if it occurs with every newsletter issue. Experts say a ratio of 80 percent informational content to 20 percent sales information is about right.

9. Stay on topic. Your readers gave you their e-mail address so they could learn more about topics related to protecting their valuable home while they're away and other related topics. Stay away from personal topics, as some will enjoy learning about your personal life, but an equal amount will not care, and be inclined to hit the spam button or unsubscribe.

10. Also, post your newsletters on your website or blog so readers can find them at a later date. In addition, the search engines will spot and index them, and help steer new prospects to your site.

## Your Own Home Care Website

A simple website is the best way to advertise your senior homecare business. A website is the new 21$^{st}$ century version of traditional

Yellow Pages advertising, because most prospects expect to find your business, or any other business, on the Internet.

If you think putting up a website is expensive, think again. The cost of hosting a website has dropped over the last few years, so today you can get high quality hosting for under $10 a month, with all the bells and whistles that used to be expensive add-one, now included for free with hosting.

## Three Reasons Your New Senior Home Care Business Needs a Website

Today, a website is an essential marketing tool for any business, and even more so for a senior service business. Whether you provide in-home senior care, senior transportation, senior concierge services, or senior relocation services, a simple website can help you find new customers and stay in touch with existing clients.

A website can help you build your senior service business in 3 ways:

- Market your senior service to new prospects.
- Educate consumers about your services.
- Help prospects and current customers contact you.

If you're new to building a website, make a list of what you want to accomplish before building your site. For example, do you want to make it easy for new prospects to learn more about your services before they contact you? How about a page that contains a sample service agreement that customers or prospects can read or print?

Most basic senior service websites include a FAQ page that contains all the frequently asked questions and answers about your senior services, a contact page with both phone and email contact information, a page listing the services you offer, and, after you have them, testimonials from satisfied customers. It can be helpful to visit other senior service websites to see what others are doing as well.

If you are like most new business startups, your advertising/ marketing budget is tiny. Why not harness the power of the Internet to build your business, without spendings a lot of money, by signing up for website hosting with one of the companies that offers not only affordable hosting services, but also free help to create your website?

You may have heard about hosting companies that offer free hosting, but here's why you should only consider paid hosting for your senior service website:

1. You can use your own domain name, such as "dependableseniorcare.com". When you have registered your domain name, you own the name, which can help your search engine visibility when prospects search for a senior care business.

2. Paid web hosting is very affordable, and you will get better tools and resources to help you create and maintain your website.

3. More design options. Using paid hosting will allow you to choose the best design, or "theme," for your site, instead of the limited choices from free hosting services.

4. No ads. Free hosting companies may place ads on your website. That's how they make money, even though your website hosting is technically "free."

I'm a big fan of WordPress to build a website. Although it started as a blogging program, WordPress has now become a capable, yet user-friendly site builder that can be customized to meet the needs of almost any senior service business.

With thousands of free themes and free help from a huge online forum of users, it may be the best way to build an affordable website. In addition, there are thousands of "widgets" and "plugins" that can be added to your website to provide additional features like videos, shopping carts or customer surveys.

Even if you're not a tech-savvy person, setting up, maintaining and adding to your site is easy enough for most users to do themselves. If you do need help, sites like elance.com and odesk. com can provide affordable, knowledgeable pros to help.

I use SiteGround for my website hosting, because it's so easy to use, with a free domain name, 1-click automatic WordPress installation, free email accounts, and great customer service by phone, chat or email 24/7. I highly recommend SiteGround for your website host and have been happy with their service for several years. **www.siteground.com**

## Sample Senior Care Website

A basic website for your senior home care business should contain five essential pages to start, then you can add more as needed. You may adapt the information listed below to use for your own website.

### Home Page/Welcome Page

The home page of your website is the first page a visitor will see. Use the welcome page to provide a brief overview of your business. Here is a sample of text you could use for your welcome page:

Welcome …

*"Your Company Name"*

Affordable, Compassionate Care for Seniors.

You can trust us for senior non-medical home care and companionship services.

Thanks to improved medical care, more seniors are living well into their 80s and 90s. Many are capable of maintaining their independence at home with some outside help and assistance. That's what we do.

We help seniors stay in their own home and enjoy an independent life. At home, surrounded by familiar things, seniors experience less stress and live happier, healthier, longer lives.

**Our Simple Mission …** Our caring and capable non-medical home care services for seniors help our clients live a safe and independent life in their own home. We provide peace of mind – at no extra charge!

To learn more about what we can offers, click on "our services" in the menu bar above.

## About Us Page

_Your Company Name_ was founded by _Your Name_ *(put your photo here.)*

To provide high-quality non-medical services to seniors in _Your Town_. – seniors living alone who are at great risk for falls, medication errors and mental stress from loneliness and isolation.

We Respect Your Privacy ... We help seniors stay safe and happy in their own home – at affordable prices. All information about our clients and their families is kept strictly confidential.

We are Licensed, Bonded and Insured to protect our clients. Our rates are reasonable and affordably priced at only _____ per hour. Our rates reflect high-quality caregiving. Shopping for the lowest price may be okay for groceries, but not the services of a trained caregiver. Remember ... Hiring a "bargain" caregiver can be a risky decision that far outweighs the money you might save.

Our caregivers are active, semi-retired people who love helping others! Mature caregivers are more in touch with the needs and desires of seniors. They are patient and positive, with great people skills. In addition, they are dependable, honest and caring. For you, this translates into peace of mind, and the highest quality of service.

## Our Senior Care Services

*Your Company Name* provides affordable solutions to seniors who need assistance with their daily activities. We can help you and your loved ones with a wide variety of services, such as:

- ✓ Errands and grocery shopping.
- ✓ Home safety checks.
- ✓ Light housekeeping.
- ✓ Meal preparation.
- ✓ Medication reminders.
- ✓ Personal care assistance.
- ✓ Transportation to appointments.

These personalized services are available 7 days a week and can be customized to meet individual needs.

Our services are a perfect solution for seniors who are not ready to leave their home.

Give us a call today to discuss your needs and questions.

*(Your phone number here)*

## Contact Us Page

Simply list your contact information on this page or use something more formal. I use a free WordPress plugin called the "Fast Secure Contact Form," which, just as the name says, prevents spammers from sending junk mail to your email inbox.

## Website resources page

### Alzheimer's

The National Alzheimer's Association has several helpful free guides to coping with Alzheimer's disease, ranging from the basics to caregiving to safety, treatments and "Know the 10 signs of Alzheimer's."

(www.alz.org/alzheimers_disease_publications.asp)

The Alzheimer's Foundation of America provides a wide range of publications about Alzheimer's, as well as a free hot line (866-232-8484) for caregivers, staffed by social workers.  www.alzfdn.org

### Elder Abuse

The National Center on Elder Abuse (www.ncea.aoa.gov) offers a variety of helpful resources to educate the public and assist victims of elder abuse, including links to local hotlines and prevention programs.

## Fall Prevention

The U.S. Consumer Products Safety Commission (www.cpsc.gov) has put together a free booklet on *"Safety For Older Consumers – Home Safety Checklist."* That covers all the essentials needed to prevent falls and accidents in and around the home.

## Fraud & Identity Theft

When it comes to elder fraud, why not learn from the top dog – the FBI. At their senior citizen fraud page, you'll find a comprehensive list of the most common frauds and scams, from telemarketing fraud, identity theft, advance fee schemes, investment scams, internet fraud, reverse mortgage fraud, even counterfeit prescription drugs, and how to protect yourself or your loved ones. www.fbi.gov/scams-safety/fraud/seniors

---

# What to Do When A Prospect Calls You

Prospect inquiries are the fuel for your senior care business because they turn into paying clients to help grow your business income (And the income of other members of your LLC co-op, if you take that approach)

Most of your inquiries will be phone calls from prospects who spotted your ad on Craigslist, found your website, or heard about you from a happy client or other senior care professional.

It's important to make yourself available, so use a cell phone number in your ads, or forward your landline/voicemail to your cell phone when you will be away from the office.

If your phone has caller ID, and you don't recognize the name, introduce yourself professionally. For example: *"This is Nicole, with Dependable Senior Care … May I help you?"* Once you have determined the caller is a prospect for your service, try to get their contact information: *"May I have your name and number in case we get disconnected?"*

Keep the New Prospect Form handy, so you can use it to get all the information you'll need to decide if you can help the prospect, and the rate you will quote them. After you have filled out the form, pre-qualify the prospect: *"Is this rate within your budget?"* You'll often find that folks have no idea what the cost of high-quality home care is, and simply can't afford it, or afford as many hours as are needed.

Often a prospect will let you know that other providers have lower rates. Here's what to tell them: *"With senior home care, lower rates can mean lower quality. A lower priced provider may not have insurance or be bonded. You do want the best care for your mom … Right?"*

If a prospect is still interested, set up an appointment to discuss their senior care needs and options, and fill out an assessment form at the meeting. You'll find that form in the back of this guide.

If your prospect brings up cost again, explain the risks of hiring a cheaper caregiver:

✓ The caregiver, if not licensed, bonded and insured, becomes the client's employee.

- ✓ If the caregiver is injured on the job, homeowner's insurance will not cover it. Medical expenses can quickly grow to thousands of dollars.
- ✓ If the caregiver is an employee, the client is responsible for payroll taxes on their wages.
- ✓ If a caregiver steals something valuable, there is no bond to pay for their dishonesty.

## Follow Up with Prospects

Prospects need a reminder that builds on your conversation during the interview. For example, a phone conversation might go like this:

> "It was good speaking with you last Friday, Mr. Smith. I could tell you were looking for the best possible assistance for your mom. That's our specialty – high quality care that helps our clients live an independent life. Thanks for making time in your schedule to learn about our services. If I can help in the future, don't hesitate to call me."

You can convey the same message with a postcard or a letter, but don't send an email, as most people feel it is too impersonal. A simple follow-up is a time-tested, proven, technique for winning new clients, and the cost is next to nothing.

## Scheduling

Organizing your work schedule is simple if you do not have employees. Most of your clients will need 3-4 hours per day and 3-5 days per week, so you can help several clients at once. If you have clients that require less attention, say 2-3 hours a day, or brief "safeguard visits," you could help several clients in a day.

An occasional new prospect may inquire about live-in care, but that means you won't have time for any other clients, so think carefully about accepting live-in assignments.

If a new client needs your help, you may have to say no, or work fewer hours than the new client would like. That's why a small co-op of caregivers operating under the LLC business umbrella might make sense for you if you don't want the headaches and responsibilities of managing dozens of employees.

This arrangement can help ensure that new clients can be served by one of the co-op members, rather than being turned down or referred to another care giving business.

To ensure that you have steady work and a full schedule, you can require a minimum of 4 weeks for new clients, together with a 1-week notice, so you can find a replacement client. By using the online referral companies mentioned earlier, or Craigslist, you should have no trouble staying as busy as you want.

Using an online scheduling program or calendar can really simplify your record-keeping, whether it's just 3 clients or a dozen employees to track. Here are a few options for a small home care business:

**Appointy.com** – This free service works with Google Calendar, also free.

**Setmore.com** – Another free service, which allows up to 20 employees and unlimited appointments.

**GoDaddy.com** – Their bookkeeping service, mentioned earlier, includes free scheduling and invoicing as part of the package. Just click on the total hours, and an invoice is generated, ready to send to your client. You can even set up automatic reminders for late payers!

**Google Calendar** – If you are doing your own billing, just download the free calendar from Google (www.google.com/calendar) to schedule and track your hours and appointments.

## Getting Paid – Cash, Check or Plastic?

If you are working directly with a client who is paying the bills, ask them what payment method they would prefer. Many seniors are a bit old-fashioned and prefer to use cash or a check to pay.

Many clients rely on their adult children, who may live far away, to pay the care giving bills. For them, as well as seniors paying their own bills with a credit or debit card, you should offer a way to accept a charge card. I recommend using a credit card processor that does not charge a monthly fee as that can cut into your profits. Two companies that I recommend (and use daily), cater to small businesses, and charge affordable rates.

**PayPal.** This company is the largest in the world, yet still offers excellent customer service. Your clients can easily pay their bill, and the payment goes directly to your account.

**Propay.** Using the Propay credit card reader on your smart phone you can swipe a client's credit or debit card on the spot or enter their credit card information online.

# CHAPTER FOUR

# Understanding Seniors

We all grow old, and as we do, we experience changes to our bodies and minds that affect our abilities, behavior and personality. The speed at which we age varies greatly from person to person, as does our ability to handle aging.

Biological loss is the aging of our physical body, which is caused or influenced by a variety of factors, such as heredity (the genes we inherit from a parent), wear and tear, weakened immune system, and a variety of chemical and structural changes in the body.

## Functional Loss

As we age, we experience functional loss, which can make us more dependent on others. Functional loss includes:

- ✓ Falls and other injuries.
- ✓ Hearing loss.
- ✓ Illness, such as cancer or diabetes.
- ✓ Loss of mobility.
- ✓ Osteoporosis – brittle or weakened bones.
- ✓ Vision issues, such as glaucoma.

You can help seniors deal with functional decline by encouraging them to do some form of exercise every day. This can be as simple as walking, stretching or lifting light weights. Always have your client's doctor review exercise plans before starting any exercise program.

Another way you can assist is to help your client prevent falls. Falls can lead to a downhill slide in a senior's overall health, especially if the fall causes a broken limb or hip. I consider fall prevention important enough to include a special home safety checklist later in this guide.

## Social Isolation

Senior's need social interaction, but as they age, it can become more difficult to meet and socialize with others. This can be caused by a loss of mobility, a chronic illness, or the loss of a spouse or loved one. Social isolation often leads to substance abuse, such as excess alcohol consumption, poor eating habits that can cause nutritional issues, and increased anxiety or depression.

You can help clients who are isolated by encouraging more social activities, community events and activities, like a visit to the local senior center for lunch. Self-esteem plays a big role here, so be positive to help your client feel needed and valued. If they are no longer able to drive, look into the local dial-a-ride service, a friend with a vehicle or even by driving them yourself.

## Substance Abuse

Excess use of alcohol or drugs can affect coordination, reaction time and balance, and make seniors more prone to falls or other injuries. Also, as we age, our bodies process both alcohol and medications differently than when we were younger, so what have might have been okay at fifty could be fatal at seventy-five.

Causes of senior substance abuse include health issues, financial issues, moving, retirement, death of a spouse or friend and loneliness. A senior may also drink or abuse prescription drugs to calm nerves, numb pain or reduce depression.

Be alert to the possibility of substance abuse, especially if a client is mixing alcohol with prescription drugs that could interact with alcohol. If you see signs of a problem, contact the client's primary care doctor, or another health care professional who may be able to help your client.

## Depression

This condition is quite common in seniors, and can produce suicidal thoughts, a loss of interest in activities, a loss of energy or enthusiasm, difficulty in making decisions, difficulty in sleeping, even weight loss.

If you suspect a client is experiencing depression, (look for lethargy, sadness, withdrawal, and neglecting personal appearance and hygiene) do not try to cheer them up. Instead, pass your observations on to family members or someone on the client's care team, such as their doctor or other health care professional.

## How to communicate with your senior clients

Communicating with seniors can often be challenging, as the elderly may have physical or mental issues that require more patience and compassion. But is essential to learn the basic communication skills so you can understand and help your clients. Here are six essential tips to focus on:

1. Use open-ended questions that require more than just a yes or no answer. You will learn more from your clients if you take this approach.

2. Sit face-to-face, which gives your clients the feeling you think they are important. Many older people have hearing loss and rely on lip-reading to understand what you are saying.

3. Pay attention to make sure your client understands what you are saying. If they don't seem to understand, rephrase it instead of repeating it. Do not speak louder.

4. Maintain eye contact to pick up non-verbal hints, and touch when appropriate.

5. Show interest in what your client is saying, even if you've heard it many times before.

6. Instead of telling your clients what to do, show them.

## Listening

Listening can be just as important as speaking when communicating with clients. Try these techniques with your clients:

- Be respectful of your client, and non-judgmental.

- Try to be aware of when to stop listening and start talking.

- Listen without speaking when dealing with angry or upset clients.

- Maintain eye contact, and avoid distractions, like your cellphone.

- If you don't understand what they are saying, ask for clarification.

- Don't cross your arms – it sends the message that you have already made up your mind.

## Are you guilty of "Elderspeak?"

Many caregivers, often without even realizing they are doing it, use "Elderspeak," or baby talk aimed at seniors. It implies that the senior is incompetent, frail, dependent or child-like, and that all seniors suffer from memory or hearing problems.

Here's how to spot Elderspeak:

- ✓ Speaking slower or louder than normal.
- ✓ Using a sing-song voice.
- ✓ Using "we" and "our" in place of "you." For example, "How are we doing today?"
- ✓ Using cute names like "honey," "dearie," or "sweetheart."
- ✓ Answering questions instead of asking them. "You would like your lunch now, wouldn't you?"
- ✓ Shortening or simplifying sentences.

Eldercare experts have found that when seniors are exposed to Elderspeak, they feel that people are talking down to them, which can cause them to get angry, refuse to cooperate, even cause depression.

Using Elderspeak with your clients can trigger feelings of incompetence, decreased self-esteem, withdrawal or anger. To avoid Elderspeak, begin a conversation by asking the client what they would like to be called, and respect their age and elder status. Pay attention to the way they react to your language. Avoid terms of endearment, such as "sweetie." Here are two examples:

**Elderspeak:** *"Good morning honey. Are we ready for our bath?"*

**Respectful:** *"Good morning, Mrs. Smith. Are you ready for your bath?"*

**Elderspeak:** *"Hi sweetie. It's time for our exercise today. Let's get ready to go for a walk."*

**Respectful:** *"Hi Mrs. Smith. It's time for your exercise today. Let me help you get ready for your walk."*

A recent study by Dr. Becca Levy found that seniors who had a positive attitude about aging lived an average of 7 years longer – a larger increase than for exercising regularly or not smoking! You can help them retain that positive attitude by avoiding Elderspeak and boosting their self-esteem whenever possible.

If you want to help your senior clients live a longer and happier life, watch your words, as they can be very powerful in both positive and negative ways, and never call one "sweetie."

## Difficult Clients

Most senior home care clients are grateful for your assistance, and easy to be around. Unfortunately, you will encounter the occasional difficult client, and must deal with them in a way that enables you to do your job effectively. Here are a few tips for handling difficult clients:

1. Don't take it personally. Your client's behavior is a reflection on where they are at in life. Being elderly or sick or frail can be scary, and that can affect how they interact with you.

2. Set boundaries. When necessary, teach your clients how to treat you today and in the future. For example: "I treat you respectfully, and I expect the same in return."

3. Acknowledge their feelings. You don't have to agree, but just let them vent their feelings. This will help them feel valued and appreciated.

4. Hold your ground. Difficult clients are often in love with their misery and suffering and will dial it up a notch or two if you give in to them.

5. Use fewer words. Difficult clients tend not to listen so don't go on but respond with short sentences that are easy to understand.

## Safeguard Visits – the ideal "add-on" service for your senior home care business.

For every senior that requires regular home care, there are many more who could use a "safeguard" visit at least once or twice a week. These seniors are usually living independently at home, and for the most part, able to take care of their day-to-day needs without daily help.

Seniors living alone risk falls and other accidents, mental stress due to isolation, loneliness, and medication errors. Many do not have family living nearby, such as adult children, who could visit their parents regularly. Many adult children live too far away to visit and need a "surrogate" son or daughter to visit their elderly parent or parents.

This is where you can help. By offering regular safeguard visits, you can ensure the senior's home is checked for fall safety, (you'll find a checklist in the resources chapter) and that they are doing well.

After each visit, you can call or email the relative who requested the safeguard visits to let them know that their parent is safe and secure. This simple, yet powerful service can bring so much peace of mind for those who are unable to visit regularly.

A safeguard visit lasts about a half-hour, and you follow a simple checklist that includes the following areas, plus any items that a relative may ask you to check:

✓ Personal safety check. Take a quick look around to see if there is anything that could cause a fall or other accident.

✓ Observe appearance and demeanor – any changes from the last visit?

✓ Monitor medications – make sure your client is taking their medications as required.

✓ Check room temperature and adjust thermostat if necessary.

✓ Companionship. Sit down with your client and talk about what's happened in their life since the last visit, and what they have planned for the coming days. Find out if there is anything you can do for them in addition to the regular safeguard visit.

Because this is a short visit, and you'll need to allow for commuting time to and from the client's home, the cost is higher than your normal hourly rate. For example, if you visit for a half-hour, spend ten minutes each way driving to their home, and five minutes emailing your findings to the client's relative, you'll have about an hour invested.

A customary rate for a safeguard visit is the hourly rate, plus 50 percent. For example, if you normally charge $24 an hour, a safeguard visit would be billed at $36.

As most of your new clients will do a web search to find you, it is essential that you have a website to help them do that. You'll find a sample website earlier in this guide to help you set up your own. Be sure to list the name of your town on the home page so the search engines can include your site in any listings for your town.

# CHAPTER FIVE

# Senior Home Care
# Business Forms

These are the essential forms needed for a home care business. They are ready for you to customize and adapt to your specific requirements. To make sure these forms are legally binding in your state, we recommend you have an attorney review any forms you use in your business to ensure they meet your needs and any legal requirements in your state.

---

## Service Agreement

This agreement is entered into between _____
_____,
hereinafter called "Service Provider" and _____
_____, hereinafter called "client."

Client's address _____.

Client's phone number _____.

Client's email address _____.

The service provider agrees to provide the following services to:

Client _____

Date _____

Service address _____

- ✓ Caring companionship
- ✓ Light housekeeping
- ✓ Meal preparation
- ✓ Medication reminders
- ✓ Assistance with personal care
- ✓ Incidental transportation

Client is aware that service provider provides non-medical services only and is not licensed to provide medical care.

Client agrees to pay service provider at an hourly rate of $_____.

Weekend hours are an additional $_____ per hour. National holiday hours are time and one-half the regular rate. The rate is based on caring for one person.

Use of care provider's vehicle for incidental transportation will be billed at _____cents per mile when the caregiver is driving at the request of client, but not for commuting to and from work.

Service provider will bill client weekly. Client agrees to pay service provider on receipt of the invoice.

A deposit equal to the amount of two weeks estimated service is required when this agreement is signed. This deposit will be held until service ends.

Client agrees to provide at least one-week advance cancellation notice. If client does not provide notice, they will be invoiced and responsible for the normally scheduled visits.

Service provider may cancel without notice for non-payment, or if they feel the care provider is at risk.

## Weekly Schedule

| DAY | START TIME | FINISH TIME | TOTAL HOURS |
|---|---|---|---|
| MONDAY | | | |
| TUESDAY | | | |
| WEDNESDAY | | | |
| THURSDAY | | | |
| FRIDAY | | | |
| SATURDAY | | | |
| SUNDAY | | | |

Client signature_____

Date_____

Financially responsible party? _____

(If other than client)

Service provider signature _____

Date _____

# Client Assessment

*Your Company name, address & phone number...*

Today's date _____ Start date _____

## Personal Information

Client name _____

Phone _____

Client address _____

Client age_____ Date of birth _____

Primary care physician_____

Phone _____

Emergency contact #1 _____

Relation _____

Home phone _____

Cell phone _____

Emergency contact #2 _____

Relation _____

Home phone _____

Cell phone _____

| Diet Restrictions | Food Allergies |
|---|---|
|  |  |
|  |  |
|  |  |

| Medical Conditions / Diagnosis |
|---|
|  |
|  |
|  |
|  |

| Medications |
|---|
|  |
|  |
|  |
|  |

## Personal Information

**Disability history:** What caused need for home care?

Other In-home caregivers?

Name _____

Phone _____

Children? _____

Visitation Frequency? _____

Pets? _____

Pet care required? _____

Veterinarian? _____

Phone _____

Able to drive? _____

Special needs? _____

# Non-Medical Plan of Care

Client name: _____

Age: _____

Address: _____

Phone: _____

## Companion Care:

- Reading  _____
- Exercise  _____
- Alzheimers/Dementia _____
- Meal preparation _____
- Light housekeeping _____
- Laundry  _____
- Medication reminders _____
- Transportation  _____
- Other  _____

## Personal Care:

- Bathing _____
- Dressing _____
- Elimination _____
- Oral care _____
- Walking  assistance _____
- Other _____

## Safety:

- Check walking areas for risks_____
- Emergency Alert Okay?_____
- Equipment check (wheelchairs/walkers ?) _____
- Smoking/Alcohol _____
- Pet care _____
- Mental state? _____
- Hearing issues? _____
- Vision?_____

## Proposed schedule:

Monday: _____ Tuesday: _____

Wednesday: _____ Thursday: _____

Friday: _____ Saturday: _____

Sunday: _____

# CHAPTER SIX

# Growing Your Business

## Setting Goals

Goal setting is at the top of my "must-do" list for business success. Setting goals helps you think about your future and close the gap between where you are now and where you want to be next year or even further into the future.

The key to goal setting success is writing your goals down on paper. Just the act of writing them down makes them seem real and make them part of your new reality. Get started by writing all the goals for your new business as if you were guaranteed to succeed no matter what.

Think about what you really want, no matter how impossible it may seem to you now. Take some time to dream big! Next, list your goals in order of importance and pick your most important goal. Then ask yourself "What one small step can I take to get me closer to that goal." Then do it today, no matter how small it may seem to you. Just getting started is what counts.

***"A goal without a plan is just a wish."***

Never forget - every goal, large or small, can be achieved by taking tiny steps every day toward that goal. Breaking your goal into smaller steps can build momentum and reduce the pressure of trying to deal with large goals.

Starting a new business is a large goal, and can seem overwhelming at first glance, but by breaking it down into small daily steps, it becomes much easier and not so overwhelming.

## Action Steps:

1.  Write down what you really want.
2.  Write down how you'll get there.
3.  Write down your first step towards your most important goal.

> *"Find something you love to do, and you'll never have to work a day in your life."*
>
> GROUCHO MARX

## Setting Realistic Goals

If you don't feel you can reach a goal because it seems overwhelming or you doubt your ability to achieve the goal, it's time to break it down to more manageable "mini-goals."

For example, if your goal of making $100,000 yearly in 2 years with your new business seems too big, break that goal into smaller goals. Set monthly goals, a 6-month goal, and a 1-year goal that are smaller and easier to achieve.

# Deadlines

### *"A goal is a dream with a deadline."*

It's important to set deadlines for your goals and the smaller steps to reaching the big goal. For example, say you'll contact 10 potential new customers by October 30th. As you meet your deadlines, you'll build self-confidence and strengthen your belief that your goals are within reach.

## Action Step:

Write down deadlines for all your goals - large and small.

### *"Most people overestimate what they can do in one year, and underestimate what they can do in ten years."*

BILL GATES

Most of us are too optimistic when setting goals and making plans. That's why it's not uncommon for things to take longer than expected. If that happens, don't quit or give up! Stick with your goal and realize that you WILL get there, even if it takes a while longer than you thought.

## The 80/20 Rule

In working toward your goal, you'll find that 20% of your efforts will bring 80% of your progress towards that goal. This rule may not seem logical, but it has proven to hold true across a wide variety of situations and businesses.

That's why it's important that you find the things that will have the most impact and spend more of your time on them. Here's how to find your personal top 20%:

Make a list of all the things you can think of that could help you achieve your goal. Aim for at least 10 things, 20 is better. Next, ask yourself, "If I could only do one thing on my list, which one will help me the most in reaching my goal?" Now go through the list again and identify the second item that will help you the most. If your list has 10 items, the top 2 gives you your 20%.

## Daily Actions

When you work on your goal every day, you'll see progress and help make your goal a reality. By taking small steps every day, you'll feel like your goal is closer and it will empower you to push on.

We all have busy lives, so it's important to set aside enough time each day to work on your goals. Just do what is comfortable at the start, and pledge to stick to it. As you become more at ease with your new daily routine, you can spend more time on it.

> *"You cannot change your destination overnight,*
> *but you can change your direction overnight."*
>
> JIM ROHN

If you think you don't have enough time in your day to start a new business, you need to identify the distractions in your life and avoid them or get them under control. Some examples: Turn off your technology alerts! When you need to focus on starting and growing your new business, turn off your email, phone, social media and chat.

Next, stop watching so much television, especially the news. The average person now spends several hours a day watching TV, and you can put that time towards growing a profitable business and a better life. Don't let these distractions control you!

## Limiting Beliefs

*"Success is nothing more than a few*
*simple disciplines, practiced every day."*

Limiting beliefs can hold you back and create a false reality that can keep you from succeeding in your new business. The most common limiting belief when you're starting a new business is "It's too difficult" or "I'm not smart enough."

These limiting beliefs can cause you to put things off or quit at the least sign of failure or difficulty. Having these negative thoughts is normal, but never allow them to prevent you from moving forward.

When you have negative thoughts, give yourself permission to let them go. Replace these negative thoughts and limiting beliefs with more positive and empowering ones. Instead of "I can't do this," use "My new business will allow me to have a life I love."

## Visualize Your Success

Imagination is one of the most powerful tools for improving your life and increasing your odds of business success. The more you visualize your goals, the more confident you'll become about your ability to reach those goals.

Take a few minutes every morning to visualize your goals and imagine how you will feel when you reach those goals. This will give you confidence and empower you to continue to take the steps necessary to reach your goals.

## Action Steps

1. Focus on positive visualization every day that encourages action.

2. Remove negativity from your life and focus on the positive side. Your glass is half-full, not half-empty!

3. Every day, imagine your business is a huge success, and be confident it will be.

*"For things to change, YOU have to change. For things to get better, YOU have to get better. For things to improve, YOU have to improve. When YOU grow, EVERYTHING in your life grows with you."*

JIM ROHN

## Networking - How to Do It Right

Networking is the most effective way to build your senior transportation business. It cost almost nothing - just your time. It's about building relationships with others with the goal of mutual benefit. It's more than passing out business cards. Networking is a two-way street, not just about trying to get something out of someone.

Networking is also about building trust. People always prefer to buy a product or service from someone they know, like and trust. Think about it. Would you rather let a stranger drive your senior parent to the doctor's office or get it done by someone recommended by a friend or business associate?

Yet, if you're shy like me and so many others, just the thought of networking can be intimidating. When networking, remember you are building relationships, not make a sale. Here are a few proven tips to get you started:

1. Be genuine. Don't try to be someone else. If you're not a natural extrovert, that's perfectly okay.

2. Networking is about making friends. If you've ever made friends, you know how to network.

3. No one cares about you. All they care about is themselves. That's why you need to give something to other people you meet, whether they're potential customers or existing clients, without expecting them to do something in return.

4. When you give something to others, it creates an unspoken, often subconscious, need to return the favor. That's why networking works so well.

5. Be visible. Networking is a contact sport and the more people you contact and become visible to, the more you will build your business through networking.

6. When you're talking with someone, listen more than you speak. Give them your full attention and make them feel important by listening to them. When you do that, they will trust, like and respect you.

7. In your conversations with others, practice your ABCs (Always Be Curious). Ask what they do, ask about their family, what they do for fun.

8. Just do it - start a conversation with someone you haven't met yet and don't forget your ABCs.

Networking is an easy way to gain exposure for your new business in the community. Groups such as the Chamber of Commerce, Rotary and Kiwanis, and other business organizations can provide an opportunity to meet, greet, and become better known. Besides groups, spread the word among related businesses, such as senior care managers.

CHAPTER SEVEN

# Resources

## Online Referral Services

If you are eager to get started right away, visit these online referral services, which, much like online dating services, match clients with caregivers. Many of them take care of all the details, paying taxes, insurance and bonding, while others simply act as matchmakers between caregivers and clients. As this field is growing so fast, new services are starting almost monthly, so be sure to also do an online search for *"in-home care referral service"* to find additional services that stated up after this guide was published.

- **www.eldercarelink.com** Each month, over 100,000 people visit this site looking for an eldercare provider. You can sign up for free. There is a small fee charged for each lead they provide.

- **www.craigslist.org** The largest provider of free classifieds, where you can post a free ad offering your services, such as the suggested ad copy mentioned earlier in this guide, or search for clients who are looking for a caregiver in your area.

- **www.carelinx.com** This service connects those in need with caregivers and handles all the tax paperwork.

- **www.care.com** This is currently the largest referral service, and also handles the tax and accounting for both clients and caregivers.

- **www.careers.careinhomes.com** Provides a link between caregivers and caregiver agencies.

- **www.actikare.com**

- **www.caring.com**

- **www.carepathways.com**

- **www.caregiver.org**

Many states now maintain an online registry of home care providers. This can be a good source of referrals for your new home care business. To find out if your state has a registry, do a web search for "your state" home care registry.

## Professional Organizations for Caregivers

**Caring from a distance.** www.cfad.org This organization provides a lengthy list of online resources to both non-paid and professional caregivers.

**Family caregiver alliance.** www.caregiver.org A part of the National Center on Caregiving, with many worthwhile resources at their web site, including a link to each state so you can explore more connections within your own state.

**Inside Elder Care.** www.insideeldercare.com Chock-full of interesting posts that help families manage and learn from their care giving experiences. Worthwhile reading if you're just getting started as a paid caregiver.

**National Alliance for Caregiving.** www.caregiving.org Lots of excellent resources here for caregivers, including free webinars.

**National Association for Home Care.** www.nahc.org This organization helps for-pay home care businesses, with training, lobbying for worthy legislation to help caregivers, and a useful agency locator at their web site to help consumers locate private duty home care providers by state.

**Private Duty Homecare Association.** www.pdhca.org Provides a wide range of services to members, including training, certification, networking with others in the field and a job exchange.

## Caregiver Training

Although advanced caregiver training is not currently required in most states, the training can help you gain the trust and confidence of seniors by adding credibility. Start by enrolling in a basic caregiver training course, which can usually be completed in a short time. Classes are often held in the evening, so students are able to work during the day.

The **American Red Cross** offers a Family Care Giving Program, which covers home safety, assisting with personal care, healthy eating and caring for seniors with Alzheimer's disease. Learn more about the program at: www.redcross.org then click on "training and certification.

The **Alzheimer's Association** offers several free resources for caregivers, such as *"Practice Recommendations for Home Care Professionals," "Dementia Care Practice Recommendations"* and a free weekly e-newsletter for caregivers. www.alz.org

**Ashworth College** offers online home health aide training, with 18 comprehensive modules covering everything from communication to hygiene to rehabilitation. A certificate is awarded on completion of the program, which can take as little as 4 months. www.ashworthcollege.edu

Most state home care associations have established training programs to help newcomers to the field meet state training requirements and obtain a certificate. Visit www.hcaw.org/home-care-aide-certification to get an idea of what is offered in a typical program. To learn what is available in your state, do an online search for: "home care aide training in *Your State*"

For those who may wish to also offer medical home care, an LPN training program can provide the course work. LPN programs are offered at many local community colleges, and online as well. The program can be completed in as little as 12 months. The final step is to take the NCLEX-PN exam, which will allow those who pass to obtain a state license as an LPN.

## Useful Books

If you are ready to take your senior home care business to the next level and hire employees, here are 4 books to help you get there:

Brian Pavich, of Home Care for the 21st Century, has written a comprehensive series of four guides to the home care business. They include *"Start-Up and Operations Manual," "Helping and Understanding Seniors," "Policies and Procedures Manual,"* and *"The Employee Handbook."* Learn more at: www.homecaremanuals.com

## How to Do a Home Safety Check

Falls at home are a top cause of injuries to older adults. Seniors are also at greater risk of dying in a house fire. Almost all of these injuries are caused by hazards that are easy to overlook, but also easy to fix.

By finding these hazards and taking simple steps to correct them, you can help your senior clients avoid falls and the potential for broken limbs they can cause. Using this basic checklist, you can identify potential hazards in your client's home _before_ they cause an accident. It may take a little time to do a thorough inspection of your client's home, but it could save them thousands of dollars in medical bills – even their life!

- Smoke & carbon monoxide (CO) alarms. Two-thirds of home fire deaths occur in homes without working smoke alarms. A working smoke alarm should be located on every level of a home, outside sleeping areas, and inside bedrooms. A carbon monoxide detector should be installed on every level of a home, and outside sleeping areas. You can now purchase dual alarms that protect against both and carbon monoxide.

  **Check all smoke and CO alarms once a month to make sure they are operating properly.**

- Emergency escape plan. An escape plan can improve the chances of surviving a fire or similar emergency. Identify at least one way to escape from every room – bedrooms in particular, and avoid escape routes that require the use of an escape ladder whenever possible.

- **Telephone safety.** Post emergency phone numbers near or on all phones. Use a telephone with large, lighted numbers if you have vision problems. Keep telephones at a low height so they can be reached in case of an accident that leaves you unable to stand. Keep a telephone in each bedroom in case a fire traps you there.

- **Walking surfaces.** Tripping over loose carpet or area rugs is a common fall occurrence. Falls account for over half of all emergency room visits for seniors 65-74, and three-quarter of ER visits among seniors over 75 years old.

  **All home walking surfaces should be flat, slip-resistant and free of electrical cords or any other objects that could be a tripping hazard, especially in case of an emergency or fire.**

- **Non-skid mats.** Skid-resistant surfaces are a must, especially in potentially wet locations such as bathrooms, entries and kitchens. A non-skid mat or area rug with a non-skid backing can help prevent falls in these high-risk areas.

  **All area rugs that do not have a non-skid backing should have a separate non-skid mat placed underneath them.**

- **Steps and stairways.** All steps and stairways should have flat, even surfaces and be free of objects that could pose a tripping hazard. Stair treads should have slip-resistant surfaces, such as low-pile carpeting or slip-resistant strips.

  All stairways should have a **light switch** at both the top and bottom of the stairs, and a **secure, continuous handrail** along the full length of the stair, ideally on both sides.

- **Lighting.** Seniors need more light to compensate for vision loss. Check all light fixtures for wattage, and do not use over 60-watt bulbs unless the fixture is labeled for a higher wattage. The new LED bulbs use much less electricity, so you can have more light at less cost.

For example, and "old-fashioned" 60-watt light bulb can be replaced with a 15 watt, or less LED bulb, that can provide more light. With bulb lifetimes in the 15-25-year range, a senior may never have to replace a bulb again.

- **Electrical outlets.** All outlets in potentially damp locations, such as a kitchen, bathroom, garage or utility room, and the exterior of the house, should have ground-fault circuit interrupter (GFCI) receptacles installed to protect against electrical shocks.

   **Test any existing GFCI outlets, using the built-in test and reset buttons to make sure they are working properly.**

- **Electrical cords.** All electrical and other cords should be out of the way of foot traffic paths, as they be a tripping hazard. Never put an electrical cord under a rug or carpet, as it could overheat.

   Make sure the total wattage of all appliances plugged into a standard 16-gauge extension cord do not exceed 1625 watts.

- **Kitchen.** Every kitchen should have a working fire extinguisher and a working ventilation system to remove air pollutants and carbon monoxide from gas appliances.

   A step stool should be close by to allow seniors to reach higher shelves and cabinets safely.

- **Living room and family room.** Chimneys should be inspected by a pro every year and cleaned if necessary.

Portable space heaters should be a safe distance (usually listed on the heater label) from walls, furniture, or any flammable or combustible material.

Candles or any smoking material should never be used near combustibles, like curtains or furniture.

- **Bathrooms.** Bathrooms and showers require a non-skid mat, non-skid strips, or a built-in non-skid surface and one or more grab bars.

  Bathroom floor should be slip-resistant or covered with slip-resistant material.

  Keep small electrical appliances, such as hair dryers, shavers and curling irons away from sinks and tubs.

  Bathroom electrical receptacles should all be on a GFCI circuit.

- **Bedrooms.** Keep ash trays, smoking materials, candles and other potential fire sources away from flammable materials such as curtains, bedding and furniture.

  Keep a flashlight within reach of the bed in case of a power outage.

  Keep a telephone within reach of a bed in case of emergency.

  Never cover, fold or tuck in electrically heated blankets when in use, as it can cause overheating.

- **Basements, Garages & Storage Areas.** Set water heaters to no more than 120 degrees F. to help prevent scalding burns.

Older electrical panels with fuses should be checked to make sure the fuses are the correct size. Most residential circuits are on either 15-amp or 20-amp circuits. When possible, an older panel with fuses should be replaced with a modern circuit breaker panel.

All electrical receptacles in garages, workshops and unfinished basements should be protected by GFCI circuits.

All fuel-burning appliances, such as boilers, furnaces, fireplaces, wood stoves and water heaters, and their chimneys, should be professionally inspected yearly.

No containers of flammable or combustible liquids, such as gasoline or kerosene, should be stored inside a house or garage.

Never operate a portable electrical generator inside a home, basement or garage, as they produce high levels of carbon monoxide, which can kill in minutes.

- **Home Exterior.** Porches, steps and entries should be well-lit, with a slip-resistant surface. Outside steps require a handrail on at least one side.

  Exterior electrical outlets should be GFCI protected and in a weatherproof enclosure.

  Check to be sure a senior client can safely use exterior steps. If not, suggest a ramp be installed for safety.

# CHAPTER EIGHT

# Hiring Employees

Whether you plan to hire new employees now or in the future, it's important to do it right. Because of the complexities of today's labor laws, federal and state regulations and record- keeping involved, you need to know of these requirements before you even place your first help wanted ad.

Hiring the best people for your new senior home care business will free you to focus on the "big picture" that will help you grow your business, give you a backup person who can take over when you are sick or on vacation and increase your profits as you add new customers.

After you have hired and trained your new employee, you will also gain precious time to keep learning more about your new senior home care business with workshops and seminars. You'll also gain the time to build your network of prospects which will help your business to grow.

As your business grows, you will gain new customers, but without help, you may have to turn away those new customers because you're already over-extended and over-worked! That's not good. In addition, with good help, you will serve your existing customers better.

## When Is It Time To Hire Employees?

1. Do you feel you just can't ever take a day off? Without employees, you can forget vacations or sick days. Just one employee can give you the personal time you need and deserve.

2. Are you turning down new customers? When you have to say "no" to new customers or work longer hours just to keep up, it's time to get the help that will allow you to expand your business and become more profitable.

3. Are your customers unhappy? When your customers complain about poor service, that's bad for business. It's a sign that you need to add an employee so you can spend more time keeping your customers happy. As I mentioned in an earlier chapter, the customer signs your paycheck.

4. Do you feel overwhelmed by your workload? Do you look forward to your work every day, or do you dread it? When you're stressed or unhappy about your work, it shows, and your customers will sense it. When you love your work, it shows, and a smile on your face sends a huge positive signal to your customers.

5. Do you have a life outside your work? When you neglect your personal life because you're working all the time, guess who suffers? Your family and friends. If this describes you, it may be time to add and employee and get your "real" life back!

6. You want to grow your business, but you never seem to have time to pursue new opportunities or plan your business future. Hiring an employee can give you that vital time to plan for your bigger and better home watch business.

If you found yourself saying "yes" to one or more of these six reasons, read on while we cover the right way to find and hire your first new employee.

## How To Find Good Employees

Start with a job description. To attract the right applicants, you need to write a simple job description. Focus on education, experience and "soft skills," such as a "people person" ability to organize and time management.

A G.E.D. or a high school diploma is a reasonable minimum requirement, as senior home care work requires the ability to read and write at a basic level. Also, I've found new hires with a recent military background to be excellent employees, as the military service has trained them to be punctual, courteous and eager to succeed in the civilian world.

Older folks in their 50s and 60s can also be capable drivers, especially if your working schedule is flexible. New hires with previous NEMT experience can be great hires, and they have proven their ability to do the work with another employer.

## Pre - Hiring Setup

Before hiring your first employee, you will need to determine whether you want independent contractors or employees. The main difference between independent contractors and employees is who is in control of the work, according to the I.R.S. and most states.

If a driver is responsible for their own work and scheduling, they could be considered an independent contractor. If they depend on you to supply a list of customers, scheduling, and pay, they are considered an employee. There are a lot of "gray areas" here, and laws vary from state to state, so check with your state to find out what their guidelines are.

## Background Checks

A pre-employment background check is recommended for all new hires. Better to get any bad news before you hire than after. What information you can check on depends on your state regulations, but almost all states allow a criminal background check and a drug test, the two most important checks for you to consider.

To order a background check, do a web search for "criminal background check in (your state)" Compare prices from at least 3 providers before you order a check. The U.S. Equal Employment Opportunity Commission has strict rules that must be followed if you do a background check. You must notify the applicant in writing that you intend to order a background check.

In addition, the applicant must provide a signed consent to the check. If you are ordering a credit check, the same rules apply, plus you must notify the applicant if you refuse to offer the applicant a job because of information in the credit report.

Drug testing is often included in a complete background check, especially because of the nature of this work. Just imagine for a moment what could happen if a person employed by you was involved in a serious accident while driving a senior client and was found to be driving under the influence of illegal drugs!

Your insurance company would drop your coverage, those injured could sue you and your business could go bankrupt. So just do it! According to the current federal regulations, an applicant can refuse to take a drug test, but if they do, you probably don't want to hire them, anyway.

The U.S. Civil Rights Act makes it illegal to ask about age, race, ethnicity, color, sex, religion, national origin, disabilities, marital status or pregnancy, whether in a background check, an interview or on a written application.

## Advertise Your Job

Once you're prepared, it's time to get the word out. Almost all jobs are listed on online job boards. Explore several to see which one might be the best for your employee search.

Here's a list of the larger national job boards:

- ✓ Indeed.com
- ✓ Careerbuilder.com
- ✓ Craigslist.org
- ✓ linkedin.com
- ✓ Monster.com
- ✓ glassdoor.com
- ✓ simplyhired.com
- ✓ seek.com

## Employee Record Keeping and Taxes

First job - insure your new employees. When you hire employees, you must add worker's compensation insurance. This insurance is required in all states and covers injury or illness while on the job.

For an example, if you hired a new caregiver who injured their back or slips on an icy sidewalk on the job, worker's compensation insurance pays for their medical care and wages while they are unwilling to work.

In most states, worker's compensation insurance is available through private insurance companies. Only four states, Ohio, North Dakota, Washington and Wyoming, have their own state-run insurance plans. If you're in one of the other 46 states, contact your current insurance agent or insurance broker to set up this insurance. Your agent can also add a new employee to your surety bond.

## Why Hire A Bookkeeper?

When you add employees, the quantity and complexity of record-keeping can be overwhelming. Don't make the mistake of trying to do everything yourself. Your focus should be on running and growing your senior home care business.

Few small business owners have the in-depth knowledge of accounts receivable, accounts payable and taxes, and the yearly changes in tax laws and regulations. It's better to hire a professional who has the training and skills to handle this part of your business.

It's also a form of insurance, as missing a bill or a tax filing could affect your business credit rating or result in substantial fees or tax penalties from your state or the I.R.S.

Be sure to hire a bookkeeper that can handle both taxes and payroll so they can handle estimated tax payments, 1099s for independent contractors, Form 940 employment tax forms, W-2 forms and give you a schedule of what is due and when. Unless you enjoy handling these details daily, do yourself a favor and hire a pro!

Never forget ... your time is money that can be used towards running your new senior home care business and taking it to the next level. A good bookkeeper can save you money by ensuring that you don't make costly accounting mistakes, forget to file a form or a tax payment or forget to send reminders when a customer forgets to pay their bill on time.

If you are on a tight budget, you can use one of the bookkeeping software programs covered earlier to handle the more routine tasks, then transfer the data to a pro for the rest. Quicken, for example, is widely used by bookkeepers and accountants, so sharing date with your bookkeeper is almost seamless.

## Save on Taxes

Be sure to keep track of all your business-related expenses, as they may be deductible at tax time. Top deductions include:

- **Vehicle expenses.** At the current 58 cents per mile, this is a huge deduction for most senior home care businesses. For many, the mileage deduction alone will cover the cost of a new fuel-efficient vehicle in a year or two.

- **Startup expenses.** The cost of getting your senior home care business started is usually deductible. Check with a tax guide or tax professional to get specific deductions.

- **Education expenses.** If you take classes or workshops to maintain or improve your job skills, they may be deductible. Another good reason for attending that convention in Las Vegas next January!

- **Professional fees.** Fees paid to accountants, tax professionals, lawyers, or other professional consultants are deductible.

- **Equipment.** Check with a tax pro to see if there are any special "stimulus" deductions available for the purchase of capital equipment such as vehicles and computers.

- **Interest.** If you use credit to finance business purchases, the interest is deductible.

- **Advertising.** Any marketing costs, such as a yellow page ad, a magnetic sign for your vehicle or promotional costs, such as sponsoring a little league team or buying equipment for them, is deductible.

An excellent book on the subject is *Deduct It—Lower Your Small Business Taxes,* available at www.nolo.com.

## What to Pay Your Employees

To find good employees, you will need to pay competitive wages. If caregivers in your area are making $18 an hour, you need to match that, or finding the best employees will be difficult.

To get started, go to the help-wanted job boards listed earlier and note hourly wages for drivers in your town. Jot down 10 posted rates, then divide by 10 and you've got the magic number you need to match.

While you're checking the job boards, also study the job descriptions. This will help you write an effective ad or post at the job boards. Some job boards, like Indeed, have a template you can use by simple filling in the blanks for important items like job title, start date, pay rate and required background checks.

## Thank You for Reading!

First, thank you for purchasing and reading this book. I hope it has provided both the resources and the motivation for you to start your own local senior service business. Starting your own small business is the ticket to a better life and a prosperous future, and freedom from worries about job security.

If you have a moment, I'd really love a review. Reviews are a huge help to authors, myself included. If you enjoyed this book, please take a minute or two to post a review on Amazon. Just enter the title of this book at Amazon.com, then click on "reviews," then "write a review. Thanks so much for your support!

Wishing you much success in your new business,

Made in the USA
Coppell, TX
25 October 2024

39160542R00069